THE WORLD
UPSIDE-DOWN

Comedy from Jonson to Fielding

THE WORLD
UPSIDE-DOWN

Comedy from Jonson to Fielding

IAN DONALDSON

OXFORD
AT THE CLARENDON PRESS
1970

Oxford University Press, Ely House, London W. 1

GLASGOW NEW YORK TORONTO MELBOURNE WELLINGTON
CAPE TOWN SALISBURY IBADAN NAIROBI DAR ES SALAAM LUSAKA ADDIS ABABA
BOMBAY CALCUTTA MADRAS KARACHI LAHORE DACCA
KUALA LUMPUR SINGAPORE HONG KONG TOKYO

PRINTED IN GREAT BRITAIN

ACKNOWLEDGEMENTS

I AM pleased to acknowledge the kindness and help of Professor B. L. Joseph, who supervised my research on John Gay and eighteenth-century dramatic burlesque several years ago; and of those who read and commented upon parts of my manuscript at various stages of its development, especially Mr. J. B. Bamborough, Professor D. J. Gordon, Mr. Graham Harley, and Mr. Stephen Wall. My deepest debt is to Mr. Emrys Jones, whose lectures on Comedy in Oxford in 1960 first set me thinking about the problems discussed in the present book, and who is the source of many of its best ideas; in particular, my third chapter draws freely on Mr. Jones's own suggestive reading of *Bartholomew Fair*.

Chapter Two and Chapter Five of this book first appeared in *The Review of English Studies* and *Essays in Criticism*, respectively, and are reprinted here with some trifling changes.

Wadham College
February 1969

CONTENTS

LIST OF PLATES

Justice in the Stocks

... Liberty plucks Justice by the nose,
The baby beats the nurse, and quite athwart
Goes all decorum.
Measure for Measure, I. iii. 29–31.

I

'DEFINITIONS are hazardous', said Dr. Johnson with a wise caution, writing on the subject of comedy in his one hundred and twenty-fifth *Rambler*. Comedy is a living and evolving form, always changing a shade faster than the definitions which pursue it; the wish to circumscribe comedy with a system of theoretical ideas is in itself a somewhat comic ambition, like Walter Shandy's wish to write a *Tristrapaedia* which would prepare his son for every conceivable event that might overtake him during his early life. Yet to recognize the hazards is not necessarily to fall in with the old-fashioned and somewhat magical view that comedy cannot profitably be talked about, that it exists only to be seen and to be laughed at. Like every other form of literature, comedy arouses not only an immediate pleasure but also a legitimate curiosity about the possible sources and organizing principles of that pleasure. And to explore, in particular, the comedy of an age other than our own is often to be moved not so much to spontaneous laughter as to questions about laughter. Why, we may wonder, should certain kinds of comedy ever have been thought funny in the first place; why should certain comic scenes (like certain comic stories) recur with such persistence over the years;

what, if anything, do such comedies tell us about the society which first enjoyed them; what, if anything, do they tell us about the function of comedy in general? Here, for example, is one comic situation which reappears in English stage comedy so doggedly and over such a period of time that it is likely to drive us to some speculation. It might be called the discomfiture of the judge. A scene from the fourth act of Vanbrugh's *The Provok'd Wife* will serve to show the basic pattern of joke. The scene has some interest in that it underwent rewriting some time between 1697 and 1725, probably as a result of Jeremy Collier's attack upon Vanbrugh in his *Short View of the Immorality and Profaneness of the English Stage* in 1698. Sir John Brute and his friends, at an advanced stage of a night's toping, are out walking the streets when they meet with a tailor. The tailor is carrying a bundle; in the first version of the play the bundle contains the gown of the local minister of religion; in the revised version—'to suit the delicacy of the age', as Hazlitt dryly put it—it contains the gown of Lady Brute herself. Sir John promptly puts it on; he runs into the watch; fights with them, and is overcome; and is finally led before an amazed Justice of the Peace. For some minutes the supposed Lady Brute allows the Justice's inquisition to proceed, until the questions turn to the behaviour of Sir John himself 'in the grand matrimonial point'. 'Oons!' says Sir John, 'This fellow asks so many impertinent questions! I'gad, *I believe it is the Justice's wife in the Justice's clothes.*' The line was there in the original version, but without the situational relevance to give it full comic force; with the simplest of touches Vanbrugh has now shaped the scene to a classic comic pattern, in which the dignity and inviolability of the law is suddenly subverted by a preposterous hint—its truth or falsehood hardly matters—that beneath the judge's robes is a human being as devious and as fallible as the prisoner in his custody. 'Hark, in thine ear: change places, and, handy-dandy, which is the justice, which is the thief?'

Seventeenth-century rhetoricians had a name for such a moment as this when it occurred in formal debate, a speaker's own accusation (or suspicion) being suddenly turned back against himself by his opponent: this was known as an inversion. But comic inversion may involve more than a mere verbal stroke. Consider some more discomfited judges. Ben Jonson's Justice Overdo dresses as a fool in order to spy out the enormities of Smithfield Fair, but finds himself denounced by his own wife as one of the greatest of the fair's enormities ('Mine own words turned upon me like swords'), beaten, and placed in the stocks (*Bartholomew Fair*, 1614). Richard Brome's Justice Cockbrain, out to do for Covent Garden what 'my Reverent Ancestor *Justice Adam Overdo*' did for Smithfield, follows his suspects into an inn only to be humiliated and clubbed (*Covent Garden Weeded*, 1632). Thomas Shadwell's Sir Humphrey Maggott, Alderman and Justice of the Peace, is carried off by his nephew's crew of roaring boys to an inn, and is finally thrown out again, drunk; when the crew is brought before him for sentence next morning, they remind him of the treasons he uttered in his cups the night before: 'I shall be hang'd', he exclaims, and quickly dismisses the charge (*The Scowrers*, 1690). Henry Fielding's Mr. Justice Squeezum, having had two men imprisoned for rapes they did not commit, is himself surprised in a tavern attempting to seduce the principal female witness, and must endure the rebukes of a drunkard named Sotmore: 'Fie upon you, Mr. Squeezum! you who are a magistrate, you who are the preserver and executor of our laws, thus to be the breaker of them!' (*Rape Upon Rape; or, the Justice Caught in his own Trap*, 1730). Arthur Wing Pinero's Mr. Posket, after a night of escapades, perilous falls, and long-distance running, returns in a dishevelled state to his Magistrate's Court next morning to discover that he must try his companions of the previous night—including his own wife (*The Magistrate*, 1885).

Why do we find this comic pattern so often repeated? One answer might be that such scenes, at their most farcical and primitive level, effect for us a satisfying act of comic revenge against those whose authority we habitually respect and fear; a form of comic play-acting is allowed temporarily to overthrow another form of highly serious play-acting (the administration of justice) on which the stability of society depends. Thus the police, too, become popular objects of comic retribution. Mr. Punch, in what is perhaps the most fundamental piece of comedy our society still regularly enjoys, gives thump after thump to constable after constable, and finally hangs the hangman (though originally, we are told, the hangman seems to have had the last word on this matter). John Gay's short play *The Mohocks* (1712) sketches the pattern of comic revenge equally clearly: a gang of street terrorists force the constable and watch to exchange garments with them, and then march these disguised officers of the law off for trial before the unsuspecting Justices of the Peace. Such farcically incompetent officers are the forerunners of the Keystone Cops.

Yet a scene of this kind may also suddenly modulate from farce into an altogether more complex comic mode which is at once more compassionate and more moral. In the fifth act of *Bartholomew Fair* Jonson leads us brilliantly from the farcical encounter of priest and puppet to the humanity of the play's conclusion: '. . . remember you are but *Adam*, Flesh and blood! You haue your frailty, forget your other name of *Ouerdoo*, and inuite vs all to supper.' And in *The Magistrate* Mr. Posket makes the same anguished discovery, that beneath the robes is flesh and blood: 'I am a man as well as a magistrate.' *Judge not, that ye be not judged*: such moments as these derive their particular poignancy from the wit and compassion with which they seem to recall the gospel sentences on the absurdity of fallible man's attempting to pass judgement upon his fellows. A further modulation, and we move out of the world of comedy and into that of tragicomedy, from *Bartholomew Fair* to *Measure for Measure*, where another righteous judge discovers, to his own perturbation, the man beneath the robes: 'Blood, thou art blood.' Another modulation still, and we are in Lear's world, where Christ's words (this time on the woman taken in adultery, John 8:7) are driven to a fierce, anarchical conclusion:

> Thou rascal beadle, hold thy bloody hand!
> Why dost thou lash that whore? Strip thine own back;
> Thou hotly lusts to use her in that kind
> For which thou whipp'st her.   (IV. vi. 162–5)

No man is fit to judge another, or to rule another: Lear's vision is of a tragic stalemate, with beadle and whore, justice and thief, father and daughters, husband and wife, servant and master, king and clown standing on a common level, each as good and as wicked as his fellow, each without virtue enough to command or humility enough to be subordinate. The sense of levelling and of deadlock is, for all the obvious, large differences, curiously close to that which is sometimes arrived at by comedy; we do well to remember how powerfully the two apparently quite contradictory modes of tragedy and comedy may sometimes enrich each other by reason of their mutual proximity.

Two very closely related comic principles might be said to be at work in the scenes we have just looked at. The first, more broadly farcical element arises largely out of a comic principle which Henri Bergson described as *inversion*, a term which significantly coincides with the old rhetorical term we have already met.[1] Inversion involves a sudden, comic switching of expected roles: prisoner reprimands judge, child rebukes parent, wife rules husband, pupil instructs teacher, master obeys servant. The conventions of Roman New Comedy, with its clever children, wives, and servants pitted against dim-witted fathers, pedants, husbands, and masters provided generously for comedy of this kind; and the conventions are still strong in Elizabethan comedy. Lyly's comedies, for instance, make constant use of this comic device; in *Mother Bombie* one aged father confesses to another: '. . . wee are both well serued: the sonnes must bee masters, the fathers gaffers; what wee get together with a rake, they cast abroade with a forke; and wee must wearie our legges to purchase our children armes' (I. iii. 185–8). The neat dance of the phrases creates a sense of order and playfulness which constrasts nicely with the weariness and disorder actually being described; Lyly's style continually reassures us that we are to remain within the safe world of comedy. With a similar nimbleness the two servants congratulate each other on their skill in bringing about these reversals:

> *Dromio.* His knauerie and my wit, should make our masters that are wise, fooles; their children that are fooles, beggars; and vs two that are bond, free.
> *Riscio.* He to cosin, & I to coniure, would make such alterations, that our masters should serue themselues; the ideots, their children, serue vs; and we to wake our wits betweene them all.
>
> (II. i. 5–10)

The fathers serve the children, the children serve the bond-servants, the bond-servants alone are free, lords for the day; the entire social pyramid is inverted.

---

[1] Henri Bergson, 'Laughter', in *Comedy*, ed. Wylie Sypher (New York, 1956), pp. 121–3.

The second and more complex comic principle might be described as *levelling*. Here the emphasis is not so much upon reversal of roles or the triumph of a natural underdog as upon the artificiality of all social distinctions in the face of human passion and incompetence. Fielding is one of the masters of this kind of comedy. In the great social masquerade, he writes in his *Essay on the Knowledge of the Characters of Men*, 'Nature is ever endeavouring to peep forth and show herself; nor can the cardinal, the friar, or the judge, long conceal the sot, the gamester, or the rake.'[1] Levelling comedy is comedy of unmasking, comedy which reveals unexpected and embarrassing brotherhood in error, comedy which (temporarily at least) stuns, disables, and humbles its protagonists; comedy which eyes ironically the proposition that our social superiors are also our moral superiors. Fielding's chambermaid Betty, found by Mrs. Tow-wouse in a compromising position with Mr. Tow-wouse, valiantly protests that *her betters are worse than she*: such subversive sentiments lie at the heart of comedy of this kind. *Our Betters* is the ironical title of Somerset Maugham's comedy of upper-class life. Yet it is characteristic of levelling comedy that it explodes in two directions at once. 'Zbud, I think you men of quality will grow as unreasonable as the women', protests the shoemaker to the aristocratic rake, Dorimant, in the first act of Etherege's *The Man of Mode*; 'You would engross the sins o' the nation; poor folks can no sooner be wicked, but they're railed at by their betters.' 'Had the Play remain'd, as I at first intended,' says Gay's beggar ruefully at the end of *The Beggar's Opera*, 'it would have carried a most excellent moral. 'Twould have shown that the lower sort of people have their vices in a

---

[1] 'An Essay on the Knowledge of the Characters of Men', in *The Complete Works of Henry Fielding: Miscellaneous Writings*, ed. W. E. Henley (London, 1903), i. 283.

degree as well as the rich: And that they are punish'd for
them.' And the demure Mrs. Slipslop, sympathetically
assuring Lady Booby of the likelihood of Joseph Andrews's
fondness for her, reminds her that 'Servants have flesh
and blood as well as quality.' Levelling comedy begins with
a series of apparent contrasts; between the morality of high
life ('Our Betters') and that of low life; between the corruption of the city and the pastoral innocence of the country;
between the honesty of plain-dealing and the hypocrisy of
manners; between the strength of the man in office and the
powerlessness of the man out of office; and then quickly
proceeds to demolish the entire artificial structure of contrasts: each man is as good and as bad, as powerful and as
impotent as his fellow, no place and no style of life will
assure us of strength or of virtue, we are all of us no worse
and no better than Our Betters; 'flesh and blood', we all
stand on a common level.

It is not surprising, then, that the comic dramatist should
so often find himself accused of being a social saboteur; for
such comedy characteristically represents society collapsing
under the strain of scandalous and widespread folly and
ineptitude, centred in particular in those traditionally
thought to be society's very pillars. 'If these gentlemen had
fairly represented the average ability of the Justices of the
time', remarks Miss C. V. Wedgwood pertinently of the
figure of the J.P. as represented in Caroline drama, 'it would
be hard to understand how the administration functioned.'[1]
While in real life we have many judges who are wise and
blameless, in comedy all judges are scatter-brained and
culpable; it was just this *kind* of distortion which so distressed Jeremy Collier in 1698. Restoration comedy,
Collier argued, is disrespectful to Our Betters. What right,

[1] C. V. Wedgwood, 'Social Comedy in the Reign of Charles I', in *Truth
and Opinion: Historical Essays* (New York, 1960), pp. 194–5.

he asked, has the comic dramatist to treat the clergy and the aristocracy as though they were the same as everyone else? 'And has our *Stage* a particular Privilege? Is their *Charter* inlarg'd, and are they on the same Foot of Freedom with the *Slaves* in the *Saturnalia*? Must all Men be handled alike? . . . I hope the *Poets* don't intend to revive the old Project of Levelling, and *Vote* down the House of *Peers*.'[1] Such comedy, for Collier, had political implications; he lined the dramatists up with the old political party of the Levellers. Over forty years later, Colley Cibber was to accuse Fielding of just the same indiscriminate disrespect to authority in his political burlesque plays. Fielding's plays, wrote Cibber, 'seem'd to knock all Distinctions of Mankind on the Head: Religion, Laws, Government, Priests, Judges, and Ministers, were all laid flat, at the feet of this *Herculean* Satyrist!'[2] And the long and curious debate about the dangerous effects of *The Beggar's Opera*, which stretched right through the eighteenth century, frequently laid the same charge against John Gay. Thus a writer in *The Gentleman's Magazine* for 15 September 1773 argued that despite the wit of *The Beggar's Opera*, the play

is notwithstanding very ill calculated to mend the morals of the common people, who are pleased to find all ranks and degrees, the highest and most respectable characters, brought down to a level with themselves. The Beggar's Opera is, in truth, the Thief's Creed and Common Prayer book, in which he fortifies himself in the most atrocious Wickedness, from the impunity and triumph of his great exemplar, Mackheath; and comforts himself, that, notwithstanding he may be hanged for his robbery, he is no worse than his betters.

In private life, the comic dramatist is unlikely to be either an anarchist or a leveller; Fielding (to take an obvious

---

[1] Jeremy Collier, *A Short View of the Immorality and Profaneness of the English Stage* (London, 1698), pp. 175–6.

[2] *An Apology for the life of Mr. Colley Cibber*, ed. Robert W. Lowe (London, 1889), i. 287.

instance) happened to be a magistrate himself in his later life, and was a man of generally conservative social beliefs. Yet for all their naïvety, the criticisms just quoted do manage to highlight a major technical problem which faced such a dramatist: namely, how to hint that, behind the cheerfully anarchical society which his comedy depicted, lay a colder, more upright, actual social world to whose forms, hierarchies, law, and order he personally gave assent; how to lead the comedy back from a world of cakes and ale to a world in which stewards must play their part; how to banish Falstaff and accept the Lord Chief Justice.

The dramatic formula of the judge-brought-to-justice has survived steadily into modern times: Shaw uses it in *Captain Brassbound's Conversion*, so does Stephen Spender (for tragic purposes) in *Trial of a Judge*, so too does John Mortimer in his recent play *The Judge*. Our next comic situation has not done so well; and it seems worth asking why. This is the comic triumph of wife over husband. The scene in Jonson's *Epicoene* in which Mrs. Otter assaults her husband might be taken as a savage but concise example of this situation; a situation which is given more spacious expression in countless seventeenth-century comedies of shrews and cuckolds, of scolding and horning. However cold such comedies may leave us today, their very frequency in the earlier drama suggests their one-time power to touch their audience's nerve-centre. Shrew comedy, obviously enough, thrives in a society which has fairly formalized ideas about the relative rights, dignities, and duties pertaining to the roles of husband and wife. *Epicoene* as a whole, for instance, depends for its full effect upon the premiss that a good wife should be seen and not heard. King James was no doubt expressing a commonplace of the age when he declared 'that silence was an incomparable vertue in a woman', and Volpone had good authority for his fruitless rebuke to Lady Would-be, 'that your highest female grace is silence'.[1] Jonson depends upon this received belief in order to establish the full monstrosity of Lady Haughty and her troop, just as elsewhere in the play he depends upon our agreeing that the use of contraceptives is an unnatural practice. So secure can Jonson be in his knowledge of the way in which his audience is likely to react to his talkative women, that he can afford to give some play to the other side of the question, lending the boisterous Mistress Epicoene some unexpectedly reasonable protestations that women should not be treated as though they were less than human: 'Why, did you thinke you had married a statue? or a motion onely? one of the *French* puppets, with the eyes turn'd with a wire?' Jonson himself noted elsewhere that speech is 'the only benefit man hath to expresse his excellencie of mind over other creatures',[2] and this comedy does not simply add strength to a common belief that women ought to be silent, but at points surprisingly sabotages that belief, generating a feeling of paradox, and allowing us to see the monstrosity not only of a shrew but also of the kind of wife demanded by Morose, a speechless one. Yet it is a paradox which does not finally destroy the premiss on which the play rests, that wives really ought to stay quietly in their places. It was for Ibsen's Nora to demolish that premiss, rejecting the idea of the doll-wife, and startling her husband with the simple words, 'You and I have much to say to each other.' Shrew comedy has never been quite the same since. In 1893 Shaw made a clever but unsuccessful attempt to catch the genre on the rebound. The apparent premiss of *The Philanderer* is the newly received Ibsen view, that it is only reasonable that women enjoy the

---

[1] *King James His Apophthegms* (London, 1643), p. 12; *Volpone*, III. iv. 76–8.
[2] *Discoveries*, 2031–2, in *Works*, eds. C. H. Herford and P. and E. Simpson (Oxford, 1925–52), viii. 625.

same rights and freedoms as men: the comedy's first target
is the meek and submissive womanly woman. Shaw then
springs his characteristic counter-attack, parading the New
Woman in her full absurdity, and forcing his audience back
to an old-fashioned, pre-Ibsen view of things which they
had just prided themselves on rejecting; the nonchalant,
cigarette-smoking ladies of the Ibsen Club are the Lady
Haughties of their day. The paradox which Jonson's comedy
lightly touches is that, after all, wives might indeed be treated
with a little more sense of equality; Shaw's paradox is that
they might well be treated with a little less. Shaw's paradox,
unlike Jonson's, has—for all its cleverness—an air of
uncertainty about it, which may reflect not only the uncertainty of Shaw's audiences as to the proper role of women,
but also, perhaps, the uncertainty of Shaw himself.

Meredith, we may remember, considered that comedy
flourished only in societies which permitted equal dealings
between the sexes, where men and women stood upon a
common level.[1] Whether the society which enjoyed *The
Way of the World* (a comedy which Meredith gave to clinch
this proposition) did in fact encourage a feeling of equality
between the sexes seems open to question: one might have
supposed that one of the implications of that play was that
unless women take exceedingly elaborate precautions they
may be reduced to a position of servile dependency upon
their husbands. The particular pleasure of the more successful seventeenth-century sex-comedy often seems to
arise in fact from a feeling of daring abnormality about the
behaviour of the plain-dealing and gaily triumphant heroines, who enjoy an exceptional and often temporary liberty
of speech (granted them, sometimes, by reason of their male

[1] 'An Essay on Comedy', in *Comedy*, ed. Sypher. Meredith's views were
interestingly anticipated by James Beattie in his 'Essay on Laughter and
Ludicrous Composition' (1764), in *Essays* (Edinburgh, 1776), pp. 319–486.

disguise, as in *As You Like It*), rather than one which is naturally accorded them by their society. Although Rosalind may teasingly instruct Orlando in the conduct of a lover and of a husband, we know that she must soon revert to the meeker role of wife; Celia's agonies continually alert us to the nature of Rosalind's boldness: 'You have simply misused our sex in your love-prate.' Comedy arising out of a society which has more relaxed and egalitarian views about the way in which courtships may be conducted, and about the various rights and duties and proprieties pertaining to the roles of husband and wife, is likely to lose this particular kind of excitement, and sex-comedy is likely to find rather different forms.

The same may be true of other kinds of comedy as well. If the joke about the worsted judge is still current while the jokes about shrews and cuckolds seem faded and at times distasteful, then the reason may lie partly in the relative formality in which certain roles are regarded. Judicial procedures are still conducted with a high degree of dignity, ceremony, and formality; the power of a judge is still real, and is still widely regarded with a certain fear; jokes about judges, fictions imagining the destruction of all that dignity, ceremony, and formality, are, consequently, particularly satisfying. Since the passing of the Married Women's Property Act, the relaxation of the divorce laws, and the gradual arrival of new assumptions about the ways in which wives (and, indeed, husbands) may behave if they wish, comedies about hen-pecked husbands and triumphant wives can look somewhat uninteresting. We write comedies about Our Betters when Our Betters have real power. If such comedies depict an inversion or levelling of the social ranks, this need not mean (as Meredith supposed) that a society is in fact egalitarian, nor (as Collier supposed) that its comic dramatists are intent on undermining the accepted principles of that society. It is possible to be confused by too literal and understanding of the traditional Ciceronian notion that comedy holds a mirror to the age, as Vanbrugh and John Dennis each pointed out independently, and with varying degrees of success, in their replies to the attacks that had been made upon *The Relapse* and *The Man of Mode*.[1] 'The business of Comedy', wrote Vanbrugh, 'is to shew people what they shou'd do, by representing them upon the Stage, doing what they shou'd not. . . .' This is hardly convincing either as a defence of *The Relapse* or as universal truth about comedy; yet it is a useful partial truth, for comedy does often deal in opposites, presenting, so to speak, the anti-types as well as the types of its society. The lunatic governor (such as the one who appears at the end of Chapman's *The Widow's Tears*), the incompetent judge, the mock doctor, the equivocating priest, the hen-pecked husband: such are the familiar and recurrent figures in the comedy of a society which gives a general assent to the necessity of entrusting power to its governors, judges, doctors, priests, and husbands.

II

The parallel to which we may turn is that of festival. The function of some of the comic scenes we have just looked at appears in some respects to be like that of certain kinds of periodic festivity. Max Gluckman has suggested that ritual periods of licence in primitive communities, while they may provide opportunities for temporary release from the established social order, and even for protest against it, are not normally intended to call that order

[1] 'A Short Vindication of the Relapse and the Provok'd Wife', in *The Complete Works of Sir John Vanbrugh*, ed. Bonamy Dobrée (London, 1927), i. 206; 'A Defence of Sir Fopling Flutter' (1722) in *The Critical Works of John Dennis*, ed. E. N. Hooker (Baltimore, 1943), ii. 245.

fundamentally into question, but tend instead to strengthen and preserve it. If authority should be weak—if, as in the communities Gluckman observed, the king should be a boy, for instance—the annual rites of rebellion may be suspended.[1] The same would seem to be true of all the great social rituals which involve a reversal or abandonment of everyday social positions: the Saturnalia, the Feast of Fools, the Boy Bishop, the Carnival celebrations of Catholic Europe. The Roman Saturnalia, for instance, held annually at the winter solstice, was supposed to re-enact the freedom and equality of the Golden Age, over which Saturn was thought to have reigned; all normal business and ceremony was put aside for the duration of the holiday, and masters and servants exchanged roles; the slaves sat at table wearing their masters' clothes and the *pilleus*, or badge of freedom, and enjoyed the right to abuse their masters, who served them. A society with an acute sense of the necessity of everyday social distinctions allowed itself briefly to re-enact an apparently 'ideal' state of anarchy which it had no wish to bring permanently into being.

In some parts of Greece at the present day transvestism is practised upon certain holidays (8 January is a favourite day), the women wearing men's clothing and enjoying complete rule over the men for the duration of the holiday: a sign not of sexual egalitarianism, but rather of the reverse. Somewhat similar goings-on often took place on holidays in the England of Elizabeth I. At Shrovetide, for instance,

Both men and women chaunge their weede, the men in maydes aray,
And wanton wenches drest like men, doe trauell by the way.[2]

In England today only a few customs, such as leap-year proposals and the privilege of a bride to kiss as many men

[1] Max Gluckman, *Custom and Conflict in Africa* (Oxford, 1956), Ch. V.
[2] Naogeorgus (Kirchmeyer), *The Popish Kingdome, or reigne of Antichrist* (1570), ed. R. C. Hope (London, 1880), Bk. Four, 'Shrovetide'.

as she pleases on her wedding-day, remain as slight and half-humorous relics of such festive licence in sexual matters. When more pronounced holiday reversals of social roles occur, it is normally in institutions which continue to uphold a clear and formal hierarchy: army officers still often serve their men at table once a year; and in at least one parish in England children are permitted on one day of the year to conduct a service for an adult congregation. Yet on the whole we have lost the Elizabethan sense of holiday, and, with it, something of the Elizabethan sense of comedy.

That there is a link between the practices of festival and those of comedy has been suggested by various scholars over the past fifty years. Long ago, Francis Cornford noted that the sexual reversals of *Lysistrata* and *Ecclesiazusae* (the latter involving wives dressing in their husbands' clothes) were similar to those which took place at various Saturnalian festivals (and we may recall that in *Ecclesiazusae* Aristophanes is holding up to ridicule ideas about communism and women's rights later to be seriously advanced in the fifth book of Plato's *Republic*).[1] More recently, attempts have been made, with varying degrees of success, to connect sixteenth- and seventeenth-century English drama with contemporary festive practice. Some of these attempts remain highly conjectural: one may remain unconvinced, for example, by one writer's suggestion that the moving of Birnam wood at the end of *Macbeth* be seen in terms of an Elizabethan Maying procession, with Macbeth himself playing the part of a lord of misrule.[2] Yet C. L. Barber in his book *Shakespeare's*

---

[1] Francis Cornford, *The Origin of Attic Comedy*, ed. T. H. Gaster (New York, 1961), pp. 76–7.

[2] John Holloway, *The Story of the Night* (London, 1961), pp. 65–7. Mr. Holloway does not explain how Macbeth can be at once leader and victim of the revels.

Festive Comedy has presented a sustained and, on the whole, convincing argument for acknowledging the influence of certain holiday customs upon the comedies of Shakespeare.[1] In my next two chapters I shall suggest that several of Ben Jonson's comedies, too, may profitably be seen in the light of contemporary holiday customs; and that there may be a precise connection between the patterns of social disorder displayed in the comedies and those widely known in contemporary festive practice.

This kind of discussion is exposed to two immediate dangers. The first is that of what Barber calls 'equating the literary form with primitive analogues', brutally reducing a sophisticated comedy to fit the simple pattern of a popular holiday ceremony. A fleeting reference to festivity in a play of Shakespeare or Jonson does not turn that play into a May-game. The second danger lies in the vagueness with which the term 'festive' is nowadays sometimes used: when one writer, for example, invites us to see Congreve's *The Old Bachelor* as a 'festive comedy', the term seems to have lost any precise meaning which it might once have had.[2] The term has in fact several possible legitimate meanings, which are worth distinguishing from each other. First, comedies such as Chapman's *May Day* or Jonson's *A Tale of a Tub* might be said to be festive in that they depict events which occur on a particular holiday (May Day, St. Valentine's Day), and have a strong sense of genial disorder which appears to stem very largely from the traditions of that holiday. A comedy such as *Twelfth Night*, on the other hand, while obviously sharing something of the same atmosphere, is 'festive' in a rather different sense: although it was perhaps written for performance upon a

[1] C. L. Barber, *Shakespeare's Festive Comedy* (Princeton, 1951).
[2] W. H. Van Voris, *The Cultivated Stance: The Designs of Congreve's Plays* (London, 1966), Ch. 2.

holiday, Twelfth Night, 1602, and although it contains a number of casual references to holiday revelry (cakes and ale, and a May morning), it does not depict events which occur upon Twelfth Night or indeed upon any other named holiday. One of *Twelfth Night*'s major sources, *Gl'Ingannati*, might be called 'festive' in a third, and more emphatic, sense: written for performance at the time of Carnival, 1531, by the Intronati of Siena, the play depicts events which are supposed to take place exactly at that time and place, the last day of Carnival in Siena in 1531. The comedy is designed for performance upon a holiday occasion, and takes a holiday occasion as its subject-matter.

This third kind of festive comedy takes on a particular interest when its explores the significance of the occasion being celebrated. In the seventeenth century it was widely, and not unreasonably, believed that English holidays and holiday customs derived ultimately from those of ancient Rome. So Hobbes wrote in 1651:

> They had their *Bacchanalia*; and we have our *Wakes*, answering to them: They had their Saturnalia, and we our Carnevalls, and Shrove-tuesdays liberty of Servants: They their Procession of *Priapus*; wee our fetching in, erection, and dancing about *Maypoles*; and Dancing is one kind of Worship: They had their Procession called *Ambarvalia*; and we our Procession about the fields in the *Rogation week*.[1]

'Christmas succeeds the Saturnalia', wrote John Selden likewise, 'the same number of Holy-days; then Master waited upon the Servant, like the Lord of Misrule.'[2] In 1607 the undergraduates of St. John's College, Oxford, presented a play upon Christmas Day which traced in a similar way the origin of the festivities which were that

[1] Thomas Hobbes, *Leviathan*, iv. 45.
[2] John Selden, 'Christmas', in *Table-Talk* (1689), ed. Sir Frederick Pollock (London, 1927), p. 28.

day celebrated: 'After Supp^{r.} there was a private Showe
perfourmed in ye mañer of an Interlude, contayninge the
order of ye Saturnalls, and shewinge the first cause of
Christmas-Candles, and in the ende there was an application
made to the Day, and Natiuitie of Christ.'[1] This 'application
made to the Day' is an important feature of festive drama;
it is something which is found extensively in what is probably the most obvious kind of festive entertainment, the
Court masque. Jonson's *Time Vindicated to Himself and to
his Honours*, for instance, was written for presentation at
Court upon Twelfth Night, 1623 (it was not in fact
presented until a fortnight later), and appropriately takes
as its theme the notion of holidays and the ways in
which they may most properly be honoured. Fame, the
messenger of Saturn, announces that his master intends to
hold that night a solemn revels. The news is heard by
three figures named Ears, Eyes, and Nose. Who is this
Saturn? these characters ask; is he a Lord of Misrule?
Then his revels will be an occasion for unrestrained anarchy:

> *Nose.* O, we shall have his *Saturnalia.*
> *Eies.* His dayes of feast, and libertie agen.
> *Eares.* Where men might doe, and talke all that they list.
> *Eies.* Slaves of their lords.
> *Nose.*   The servants of their masters.
> *Eares.* And subjects of their Sovereigne.   (41–6)

'Not so lavish', warns Fame. There are ways and ways of
celebrating holidays, there are kinds and kinds of freedom
and of social equality. Saturn (it will appear) is another
name for King James, whose reign Jonson had more than
once likened to the Golden Age.[2] Yet James's kingdom,

---

[1] 'An Account of the Christmas Prince as it was exhibited in the University
of Oxford' (by Griffin Higgs), in *Miscellanea Antiqua Anglicana* (1816), p. 25.
[2] *Part of the Kings Entertainment in Passing to his Coronation*, 523–32, 599–
600.

unlike Saturn's, is obviously hierarchical, and based upon a firm system of civil law; hence his reign is, and is not, like the original Golden Age. The point is one of delicate definition. Saturn's age is in some senses an ideal, yet it is an ideal which is no longer strictly imitable. The nature of the revels, and of the holiday which it celebrates, must not be misunderstood. In *Catiline* Jonson had underlined the fact that the conspirators chose to effect their plot during the time of the Saturnalia, when each household was 'Re-solu'd in freedome' and 'Euery slaue a master'—' 'Tis sure, there cannot be a time found out / More apt, and naturall.' The threat of Ears, Eyes, and Nose in *Time Vindicated* is like the threat of Catiline's conspirators; each group wishes to carry the principles of the Saturnalia permanently into everyday life. Here and elsewhere in his work Jonson takes the festive idea as a starting-point to explore questions of social freedom and social discipline, social equality and social distinction. A holiday entertainment, apparently dealing with the lightest of matters, leads its spectators gently towards more serious problems, while never offending the decorum of what is appropriate to the occasion. In the next two chapters I shall argue that certain of Jonson's comedies written for the public stage proceed in very much the same manner; that in *Epicoene* and (even more noticeably) in *Bartholomew Fair* he presents a picture of a farcical and Saturnalian society in which normal social roles are inverted, and normal social functions flouted; and that by this means he compels us to attend to questions which are far from farcical, and which are concerned principally with problems about social order; with the problems of what Jonson called 'licence' and 'liberty'.

PLATE 1

French popular art: 'La Folie des Hommes, ou le Monde à Rebours.'

III

Let's have the giddy world turn'd the heeles upward,
And sing a rare blacke *Sanctus*, on his head,
Of all things out of order.

Such is the invitation of the antimasque revellers in *Time Vindicated* (219–21). Needless to say, it is not only in festive drama that one finds such a picture of an inverted world, in which all things run 'out of order'. In subsequent chapters of this book I shall be discussing different kinds of comedy which often prompt quite different kinds of questions; yet I shall be returning continually to the question of why, and how, comedy deals with the idea of social disorder, of a world turned upside-down. 'We dread infection from the representation of scenic disorder', wrote Charles Lamb, attempting to account for the decline in popularity of the 'artificial comedy' of the previous age.[1] Lamb, it will be remembered, defended the older comedy by arguing that it provided for its audiences no more than a harmless 'Saturnalia of two or three brief hours, well won from the world', from which one returns 'the fresher and more healthy'. Lamb's defence is easily enough refuted, for it takes all too little account of the possibly serious and possibly affective qualities of comedy; Restoration comedy in particular (as I shall argue in later chapters) tends in fact to raise moral problems which cannot be neutralized by any such easy formula as this. Yet Lamb has indicated an aspect of comedy which seems to deserve closer inquiry; and the purpose of this book is to make that inquiry.

The central figure to which we shall often return is that of the world turned upside-down. This topos of *mundus inversus* is an ancient and widespread one, found very

---

[1] *The Works of Charles and Mary Lamb*, ed. E. V. Lucas (London, 1912), ii. 161–8.

extensively in popular art and literature throughout Europe from classical times.[1] It was a favourite subject for popular engravings: remarkably similar sets of illustrations of 'the world upside-down' appeared in England, France, Italy, Russia, Scandinavia, the Netherlands, and elsewhere over a period of many centuries. The most common image in these illustrations is that of a global man, looking a little like Humpty Dumpty, standing precariously on his head, and sometimes attended by a couple of jesters. There are roughly speaking three main groups of subsidiary images. There are, first, those which show strange cosmic upsets: a sun and moon shining together in the one sky, fish flying across land, men hunting on horseback across the sea. Then there are those that show reversals in the normal relationships between animals and men: an ox cuts up a butcher who hangs from a hook, fish angle for men, horses groom their masters and ride about on their backs. This is the world of *Gulliver's Travels*, in which (as an eighteenth-century chapbook on the subject put it) 'men obey, and horses rule, / And wisdom often plays the fool'.[2] The third category, and the most immediately interesting from the point of view of stage

[1] A brief survey of the history of this figure is given by E. R. Curtius in *European Literature and the Latin Middle Ages*, tr. W. R. Trask (London, 1953), pp. 94–8. For illustrations of the figure see Pierre-Louis Duchartre and René Saulnier, *L'Imagerie populaire* (Paris, 1925), pp. 12, 13, 32, 69, 293, 299; Pierre-Louis Duchartre, *L'Imagerie populaire russe et les livrets gravés, 1629–1885* (Paris, 1961), p. 36; Paolo Toschi (adaptation de Claude Noël), *L'Imagerie populaire italienne du XVe siècle au XXe siècle* (Paris, 1964). See also Maurits de Meyer, *De volks — en kinderprent in de Nederlanden van de 15e tot de 20e eeuw* (Amsterdam, 1962), pp. 427–32; Oloph Odenius, 'Mundus Inversus', *ARV, Journal of Scandinavian Folklore*, x (1954), pp. 143–70. (For these last two references I am grateful to Mr. J. B. Trapp.) Some idea of the currency of the figure in English Renaissance literature may be suggested by the frequency of its occurrence in the works of one author alone, George Chapman: see *Bussy D'Ambois*, v. i. 150–64; 'A Coronet for his Mistresse Philosophie', 5. 5–7; 'To Harriots, Achilles Shield', 113; 'An Epicede on Henry Prince of Wales', 120–7, etc.

[2] Reprinted in John Ashton's *Chapbooks of the Eighteenth Century* (London, 1882), pp. 265–72.

comedy, shows reversals in the normal relationships between people: here we see a man holding a baby or a distaff while his wife marches up and down with a stick and a gun, a pipe stuck between her teeth; two girls beneath a balcony, serenading a bashful man; a wife beating her husband; a daughter breast-feeding her mother; a son teaching his father to read; a client defending his lawyer; a servant putting his master to work.

The figure of the world upside-down occurs commonly in English tragedy, ballad, complaint, satire, etc., from earliest times. Our concern is solely with the comedy of the long period reaching from the early years of James I to Walpole's Licensing Act in 1737; with what might be called the Golden Age of English comedy. To keep one's eye on this figure as it recurs in the comedy of this period is one way of tracing the continuity of a variety of comic traditions, problems, and techniques from the time of Ben Jonson to that of Henry Fielding.

CHAPTER TWO

'A Martyrs Resolution': *Epicoene*

I

RECENT critics have taught us to see the limitations of Dryden's famous analysis of *Epicoene* in *An Essay of Dramatic Poesy*, and of the terms in which he praises Jonson's dramatic art in general. Dryden's emphasis on the realism of the play ('I am assured from divers persons, that Ben Jonson was actually acquainted with such a man', etc.) seems to have aroused dissatisfaction even in the seventeenth century—Dennis's objections to this kind of defence anticipate the better-known ones of Coleridge—and seems to be further invalidated by a recognition of the various source-material which Jonson used in the play.[1] More fundamental, however, has been the challenge to the larger idea of Jonson as a 'classical' dramatist, who adhered closely to the traditions of New and Roman Comedy, and especially to the concept of the classical unities. This idea, claimed Miss Freda Townsend,[2] was given powerful currency by Dryden, but is not true to the facts. She argued that there was reason for regarding the baroque design of *Bartholomew Fair*, with its multiple plots, as the culmination of Jonson's formal intentions; a design which has little in common with

---

[1] *Essays of John Dryden*, ed. W. P. Ker (Oxford, 1900), i. 84. Congreve's reply to Dennis suggests that Dennis was not alone at this time in considering the play as 'farce' rather than as 'comedy'. Dennis's letter and Congreve's reply are to be found in *William Congreve: Letters and Documents*, ed. John C. Hodges (London, 1964), pp. 176–85; Coleridge's brief and penetrating comments in *Coleridge on the Seventeenth Century*, ed. R. F. Brinkley (Durham, N.C., 1955), pp. 644–5.

[2] Freda L. Townsend, *Apologie for Bartholomew Fayre* (New York, 1947).

the single plots of Plautus, Terence, and Menander. In
Epicoene itself, she pointed out, it is fairer to say that there
are three related actions rather than the single action which
Dryden observed; here, and elsewhere in Jonson's dramatic
work, it seems more proper to look for 'some unity, other
than the classical'.[1] In a celebrated essay some years earlier,
T. S. Eliot had declared that this unity hardly consisted
in 'plot' at all. Although Eliot paid tribute to Dryden's
appreciation of Jonson, his own emphasis was very different;
in such a play as *Epicoene*, he said, 'The plot does not hold
the play together; what holds the play together is a unity
of inspiration that radiates into plot and personages alike.'[2]
More recently, Ray L. Heffner, jun. developed these suggestions even further in a short and perceptive essay on
Epicoene and *Bartholomew Fair*.[3] The unity of these two plays,
Heffner argued, is not so much narrative as symbolic. In
Epicoene Jonson plays intricate variations on a central symbol of noise; in *Bartholomew Fair* on a symbol of law and
'warrant'. Like Miss Townsend, Heffner rejected the traditional comparison with New Comedy, and suggested
instead a comparison with the techniques of *vetus comoedia*,
particularly with the plays of Aristophanes. In Aristophanes, as in Jonson, one finds (he claimed) 'a mingling
of fantasy and realism' and 'a comic structure centred not
on a plot but on the exploration of an extravagant conceit'.[4]
    I share with these critics a good deal of doubt about the
usefulness of discussing *Epicoene* simply in relation to
Roman or to New Comedy; a comparison with Greek Old

---

[1] Op. cit., p. vi.
[2] T. S. Eliot, 'Ben Jonson', in *The Sacred Wood* (London, 1920), p. 115.
[3] 'Unifying Symbols in the Comedy of Ben Jonson', in *English Stage
Comedy* (*English Institute Essays*), ed. W. K. Wimsatt, jun. (New York, 1954),
pp. 74–97.
[4] Op. cit., p. 97. C. G. Thayer enlarges upon the Aristophanic comparison
in his book *Ben Jonson: Studies in the Plays* (Norman, Oklahoma, 1963).

Comedy may well be more to the point, though unfortunately we cannot always be perfectly sure what Jonson meant when he spoke of *vetus comoedia*, a term which he and his contemporaries seem sometimes to have used to refer to a kind of native drama.[1] And I believe that the unity of *Epicoene* may become more apparent if the play is seen not primarily in relation to New Comedy or to Old, but rather to a kind of native drama which has been called 'festive', and which was briefly surveyed in Chapter One. As in Jonson's court masques, and also perhaps in some of his other stage plays, the decorum of the play seems to be governed by the nature of a festive occasion which the play

[1] C. R. Baskervill remarked of Jonson's use of the phrase in *Every Man Out of His Humour*, Grex 212, that it 'would naturally be interpreted at once as referring to classic comedy, and the content seems to support this interpretation. I am tantalized, however, by the question whether the reference may not, after all, have been to the older forms of English drama' (*English Elements in Jonson's Early Comedy* (Texas, 1911), p. 212). O. J. Campbell's statement that *vetus comoedia* was a term which 'the critics of the Renaissance applied to the Greek comedy which culminated in the work of Aristophanes and to nothing else' (*Comicall Satyre and Shakespeare's 'Troilus and Cressida'* (San Marino, California, 1959), p. 4) seems not entirely accurate. Jonson is clearly referring to native drama when he uses the phrase in *Conversations with Drummond*, 16. Thomas Nashe's uses of the phrase (*The Works of Thomas Nashe*, ed. R. B. McKerrow (London, 1910), i. 92, 100) suggest the existence of a well-established form derived from Greek Old Comedy but now differing from it: 'She hath been so long in the country, that she is somewhat altered.' C. L. Barber discusses these passages in relation to the May Game of Martin Marprelate in *Shakespeare's Festive Comedy*, pp. 55, 56. It is difficult to know whether Cordatus's remark in *Every Man Out of His Humour* that the play about to be presented is 'somewhat like *Vetus Comoedia*' refers, like Nashe's, to the English counterpart to Greek Old Comedy or to Greek Old Comedy itself. It is even more difficult, so rich is Jonson's word-play here on the ideas of law, liberty, and licence, to know if Jonson's remark in the Dedication of the play to the Inns of Court that the play is appropriate to the time '*when the gowne and cap is off, and the Lord of liberty raignes*' is simply a casual one or intended to invite some kind of comparison with the spirit and form of the misrule ceremonies at the Inns; ceremonies which Jonson would have known about through such friends as Richard Martin, who had been Prince d'Amour at the Middle Temple only four years before. The balance is in favour of the conventional interpretation of the phrase *vetus comoedia*, though the problem indeed remains 'tantalizing'.

depicts; an occasion which gives certain 'laws' and 'licence' —to use terms of which Jonson was fond—both to the methods of the dramatist writing the play and to the action of characters within it. I shall try to indicate the festive basis of *Epicoene* by discussing what I take to be its central action in relation to certain festive customs popular in Jonson's England. My reading of the play will, I think, lend some support to Heffner's reading of it in terms of its leading themes and symbols; but my main divergence from his approach is that I want also to insist upon the validity of one aspect of Dryden's analysis of the play to which I think he, like Eliot, does less than justice; namely, Dryden's attention to the function of plot in the play. I shall suggest, first, that Dryden was right in principle in insisting on the importance of plot in *Epicoene*, and in attempting to find a leading action for the play; and secondly that he was mistaken in saying what that leading action actually was.

II

In following Scaliger's account of the various stages in which a well-made play unfolded—Protasis, Epitasis, Catastasis, and Catastrophe—Dryden was in fact using a traditional division and terminology which Jonson had used before him.[1] Like Jonson, Dryden recognized the importance of the temporal factor in a play, of 'what happens next'. Jonson's interest in this factor becomes all the more evident if we contrast his methods with those of Marlowe. In watching Jonson's plays we seldom experience the uncertainty about the value to be attached to 'what happens next' that we may when watching, say, the second part of *Tamburlaine the Great*; the sequence of scenes is deliberate and significant, as Probee and the Boy continually

---

[1] *The Magnetic Lady, Chorus* between Acts i and ii; and elsewhere.

insist to Damplay as they watch the action of *The Magnetic Lady*:

> ... our parts that are the Spectators, or should heare a *Comedy*, are to await the processe, and events of things, as the *Poet* presents them, not as wee would corruptly fashion them. . . . Stay, and see his last *Act*, his *Catastrophe*, how hee will perplexe that, or spring some fresh cheat, to entertaine the *Spectators*, with a convenient delight, till some unexpected, and new encounter breake out to rectifie all, and make good the *Conclusion*.
>
> (*Chorus* between Acts IV and V: 10–13, 27–31)

And perhaps nowhere in Jonson's work (unless it be in *The New Inn*) do we find a greater 'cheat' than in the last scene of *Epicoene*, when Dauphine discloses, to the surprise not only of the other characters but also—one must assume —of the audience too, the real sex of Mistress Epicoene. It is a 'cheat' which some critics have held to be a flaw in the play,[1] but it is not made simply for the sake of a cheap narrative surprise. First, there is the effect which the disclosure creates: a stunned silence. Morose, paradoxically one of the most garrulous characters of the play, simply leaves the stage without saying a word; the College ladies are for once 'mute, vpon this new *metamorphosis*' (v. iv. 244), and even Truewit and Clerimont are temporarily dumbfounded. It is the last and most spectacular of a series of twists and surprises in the play which have produced either a tumult of noise (e.g. Mistress Otter descending upon her husband in IV. ii) or utter silence (e.g. Dauphine's first entrance in I. ii, Truewit's invasion of Morose II. ii. 2–4, and his return to tell Dauphine and Clerimont of the apparent success of his interview II. iv). The forward movement of the plot, with its surprises and 'cheats',

---

[1] See C. H. Herford's Introduction to the play, in *Works*, ii. 79–80; and C. M. Gayley's Introduction in his *Representative Stage Comedies* (London, 1914), ii. 117–21.

constantly enacts what Heffner sees as the main 'symbol' of the play, noise, and its opposite, silence. Plot and symbol can hardly be separated.

Furthermore, the 'cheat' of Act v of *Epicoene* finally makes evident an important fact about Dauphine: his secrecy. The idea of secrecy runs right through the play, even to the final speech where Truewit recommends to the favours of the College ladies the boy who has played the part of Mistress Epicoene, vouching for his 'secrecie'. It is the secrecy of so many of the characters of the play which results in the profusion of 'plots' (a word constantly used, and having obvious dramatic connotations): Morose's plot against his nephew, and the various plots of the three conspirators, Truewit, Clerimont, and Dauphine, against Morose, the Otters, Daw and La-Foole, and the College ladies; drawing together these various plots is the master-plot of Jonson himself. The three conspirators conceal aspects of their own plots from each other, and each is secretive to a different degree: Dauphine, the most guarded, considers Clerimont 'a strange open man' (i. iii. 1), and tells him that Truewit's 'franke nature' is 'not for secrets' (i. iii. 4, 5). The contrast between 'secret' people and 'open' people is central to the play. *Epicoene*, like Jane Austen's *Emma*, is partly an examination of the way in which certain kinds of people enjoy what Emma calls 'disguise, equivocation, mystery' (Ch. LIV), and about the various degrees to which people are outspoken or reserved, and why. Jonson's theme, like Miss Austen's, could only be fully explored by the means of a fairly complicated and surprising plot. 'Plot' is thus not simply a vehicle for theme, but actually becomes part of the theme itself. One cannot properly examine the one without the other.

And yet even if this is granted, Heffner's main objection still remains. His emphasis on the importance of theme or symbol seems to arise very largely out of the fact that there are simply too many plots in the play to make it possible to accept Dryden's view that 'the action of the Play is entirely one; the end or aim of which is the settling of Morose's estate on Dauphine'.[1] It is, he says,

> much more accurate to consider *The Silent Woman* as consisting not of a Terentian plot depending upon the delayed completion of a single, well-defined objective but of a number of separable though related actions which are initiated and brought to completion at various points in the play and are skilfully arranged to overlay and interlock,[2]

and he goes on to show how each act in the play (except the first) is centred on a separate major action. First, it should be remembered—for Heffner does, I think, allow this fact to recede—that Dryden himself goes to pains to indicate the variety as well as the unity of the play, its luxuriance of 'by-walks, or under-Plots' which distinguishes it from the single, relentlessly purposeful plots of the French dramatists; it is even possible that in defining the way in which a play can have both variety of plot and unity of action Dryden was remembering a passage in Jonson's *Discoveries* (2678 *ad fin.*).

Once this is said, however, it must be admitted that the simple financial motive which Dryden sees as the single driving force of the play is hardly prominent and seems in itself insufficient to account for the elaborately inventive actions of Morose's tormentors. Unlike *Volpone* or *The Alchemist*, *Epicoene* does not seem to be a play about the acquisition of money. It seems more accurate to see it as a play about the persecution of a misanthrope. The central fact of the play is Morose's misanthropy: his disinheriting of Dauphine is merely one of several manifestations of this

---

[1] *Essays*, ed. cit. i. 83.   [2] Heffner, op. cit., pp. 77–8.

characteristic. Even before it is known that Morose has disinherited his nephew, Truewit and Clerimont discuss and ridicule Morose's 'disease', his hatred of noise. Throughout the play this obsession is presented not simply as something that can conveniently be exploited by the wits to recover Dauphine's inheritance, but as a monstrous and ludicrous 'humour', patently symbolic of Morose's misanthropy, and ripe for punishment. There is also Morose's conviction that he is martyred by Dauphine and his company, whom he sees as 'authors of all ridiculous acts, and moniments are told of him'; it is this which persuades them that he must be made a martyr in fact: 'Thou art bound in conscience, when hee suspects thee without cause, to torment him'; it gives 'law of plaguing him' (I. ii. 9–10, 12–13, 48–9). Later Truewit tells Morose that he is persecuted for nothing but his 'itch of marriage'; the general absurdity of an old misanthrope seeking a young silent wife is as prominent as the specific consequences of disinheritance. (Clerimont declares that Truewit himself is driven on simply by a 'courteous itch' for interference: tormentor is as irrational as victim.) There is one more curious and significant fact about Morose; his hatred of festival and of festival days. 'He was wont to goe out of towne euery satterday at ten a clock, or on holy-day-eues', says Clerimont (I. i. 181–2); 'He would haue hang'd a Pewterers' prentice once vpon a shrouetuesdaies riot, for being o' that trade, when the rest were quit' (I. i. 157–9). Truewit's first plan for plaguing Morose is to draw up a false almanac so that Morose will not know which are festival days and which are not: 'and then ha' him drawne out on a coronation day to the *tower*-wharfe, and to kill him with the noise of the ordinance' (I. ii. 14–16). And later in the play Morose is to turn on his persecutors and describe them as the very children of festival: 'Rogues, Hellhounds, *Stentors*, out of my dores, you sonnes of noise and tumult, begot on an ill *May*-day, or when the Gallyfoist is a-floate to *Westminster*! A trumpetter could not be conceiu'd but then!' (iv. ii. 124–7). Each of these obsessions and acts of Morose emphasizes his absurd isolation. The leading action of the play is the breaking down of that isolation, and the punishment of misanthropy. This is effected principally through the means of a viciously high-spirited festive ceremony, which Morose is invited to endure with 'a martyrs resolution' (iii. vii. 11). The motives of the wits are neither as simple nor as sympathetic as Dryden thought; nor is the play as 'gay' and as 'genial' as it is usually said to be.[1]

If this new 'end or aim' is accepted, the play's various 'by-walks, or under-Plots' begin to take on a new relevance. For all the action of the play after iii. iv takes place within Morose's house: the exposure of Captain Otter to his wife, and the fooling of Daw, La-Foole, and the College ladies are not simply diversions but also additional torments for Morose, forming a continuous invasion of his privacy and driving him to take refuge at the top of his house, from which he descends at unexpected moments to terrify the revellers below; driving him eventually to 'run out o'dores in's night-caps' (iv. v. 3). The calm insolence with which the guests take over Morose's house ('I like your couches exceeding well: we'll goe lie, and talke there' (iv. iv. 170–1)) is not unlike that of Subtle and Face in *The Alchemist* as they take over Lovewit's house; in each case the fact that the guests almost forget that the house is not their own adds to the surprise and terror as the master returns. The episode with Daw and La-Foole in Act iv

[1] M. Castelain described *Epicoene* as 'la plus gaie des comédies de Jonson' (*Ben Jonson, L'Homme et L'Œuvre* (Paris, 1907), p. viii); for J. Palmer it was 'the most genial of the works of Jonson—the freak of a happy mood' (*Ben Jonson* (London, 1934), p. 176); C. H. Herford remarked upon its 'gaiety' (*Works*, ed. cit. ii. 76).

is rather feeble in itself, but succeeds because of its placing. The centre of attention switches temporarily from Morose— 'wee'll let him breathe, now, a quarter of an houre, or so' (IV. iv. 155–6)—to the multiple plans against Daw, La-Foole, and the ladies, and the highest point of excitement is in fact reached when Morose enters unexpectedly at the end of IV. vi with the abandoned swords of the two knights drawn in either hand. Moments such as these, which are placed with great skill in the latter part of the play, continually remind us of the way Morose is being harassed. There are no reminders of the fact that Dauphine wants his money.

The invasion of Morose's house acts out in yet another way the theme of secrecy and openness, of things done in private and things done in public. As so often in Jonson's plays, the setting takes on an almost metaphorical quality; the setting of a house or room, with its door safely shut or thrown dangerously open. In the first scene of the play Clerimont and his page discuss why the door of the Collegiates' house should be shut to Clerimont but open to the page, who is free to make himself at home with the most private things of the ladies, their beds, their gowns, their perukes. While this discussion is proceeding, Clerimont is himself dressing, with his own door evidently standing open, for Truewit enters abruptly and unannounced in the middle of the boy's song. Truewit reprimands Clerimont for spending too much of his time in private, and tells him he should give himself more to public entertainments (I. i. 34–41), just as he tells Dauphine later in the play that he must 'leaue to liue i' your chamber then a month together vpon AMADIS *de Gaule*, or *Don* QVIXOTE, as you are wont; and come abroad where the matter is frequent, to tiltings, publique showes, and feasts, to playes, and church sometimes . . .' (IV. i. 55–60). The contrast between the two ways of life, public and private, is continued in the rest of this first scene. The lady of Clerimont's song is powdered and perfumed as if '*going to a feast*'; her 'public' face and dress Clerimont distrusts, Truewit defends. Women may practise any art, declares Truewit,

> . . . to mend breath, clense teeth, repaire eye-browes, paint, and professe it.
>
> *Clerimont.* How? publiquely?
>
> *Truewit.* The doing of it, not the manner; that must bee priuate. Many things, that seeme foule i' the doing, doe please, done. A lady should, indeed, studie her face, when wee thinke shee sleepes; nor, when the dores are shut, should men bee inquiring, all is sacred within, then.   (i. i. 110–17)

What is under discussion is not simply the propriety of using Art to mend Nature, but also the propriety of doing certain things in public and others in private, 'when the dores are shut'. This is the first of several such discussions in the play, discussions which are really simply airings of opposite views which seldom reach resolution or agreement; the effect here is to create a general feeling of uncertainty about these proprieties, and about the whole relation of public and private life. This feeling is continued a little later on in the description of La-Foole, who shatters these proprieties with a gay, lunatic abandon: 'He will salute a Iudge vpon the bench, and a Bishop in the pulpit, a Lawyer when he is pleading at the barre, and a Lady when shee is dauncing in a masque, and put her out. He do's giue playes, and suppers, and inuites his guests to 'hem, aloud, out of his windore, as they ride by in coaches' (i. iii. 30–5). And when La-Foole speaks of his relatives, the La-Fooles of Essex and the La-Fooles of London—'They all come out of our house' (i. iv. 37)—his words seem to pick up one of the leading metaphors of the play; the prolific family of La-Fooles seems to spill out of a house as real as the one in which the solitary Morose confines himself.

The action of the sub-plots, as well as accentuating Morose's suffering, repeats in a minor key the major theme of the play, as private actions are exposed to public gaze. Thus Daw and La-Foole receive their kicks and nose-tweakings 'in priuate' as it seems to them, but in fact before an unseen audience of the College ladies, brought in to serve 'a priuate purpose' of Truewit. The two men are closeted at the very moment when Morose is forced to run out of his house, and their privacy is ludicrously threatened by Truewit in a way that recalls the invasion of Morose's privacy: 'Sir AMOROVS, there's no standing out. He has made a *petarde* of an old brasse pot, to force your dore' (IV. v. 224–5). Mavis's private letter to Dauphine (beginning '*I chose this way of intimation for priuacie*') is seized and read aloud by Clerimont. Captain Otter confesses—in private, as he thinks, but actually in his wife's hearing—what his wife does when she thinks *she* is in private. The drinking-match between Daw and La-Foole organized earlier in this scene by Captain Otter with his various tankards—his 'bull, beare, and horse'—and described (as Herford and Simpson note) in the terminology of bull- and bear-baiting, seems to bring the popular holiday entertainments of Southwark into the very house of Morose.

We may notice in passing the way in which Captain Otter's liberties are usually described in 'holiday' terms. The calendar days loathed by Morose are the days of Otter's glory. Before their marriage, Mrs. Otter has declared, it was only at holiday entertainments that Captain Otter enjoyed his brief moments of distinction: 'Were you euer so much as look'd vpon by a lord, or a lady, before I married you: but on the Easter, or Whitson-holy-daies? and then out at the banquetting-house windore, when NED WHITING, or GEORGE STONE, were at the stake?' (III. i. 46–50). And now they are married we are told that it is only on holidays that

Captain Otter regains his liberty; at such times 'No Ana-
baptist euer rail'd with the like licence' (III. ii. 15). This
licence Mrs. Otter describes in terms of holiday freedom:
'Neuer a time, that the courtiers, or collegiates come to
the house, but you make it a *shrouestuesday*! I would haue
you get your *whitsontide*-veluet-cap, and your staffe i' your
hand, to intertaine 'hem; yes introth, doe' (III. i. 5–9).
Appropriately, the day on which the action of the play
takes place, on which Otter gains his liberty and Morose
loses his, is a festive day.[1] It is one of the four annual quarter-
days, on which La-Foole is having his 'quarter-feast' (II. iv.
110); it is also, of course, the day of Morose's 'wedding'.

The tormenting of Morose is carried out by the simple
device of moving La-Foole's feast and his guests to Morose's
house to celebrate the wedding. At the centre of the play
is this festive invasion by the public world—rowdy,
licentious, and apparently sociably united, though in fact
divided by individual envy and plotting—of the private
world of Morose; a world he would have silent, subjected
to discipline, and solitary. The invasion exposes the absurdities not only of the private world of Morose, but also of
the public world of the revellers; it exposes, too, the disharmony that exists *between* the private and the public
worlds. This invasion begins in III. v, with Morose crying in
vain for his doors to be barred, Epicoene insisting they be
left open, and Truewit counselling Morose to 'giue the
day to other open pleasures, and jollities of feast, of musique,
of reuells, of discourse: wee'll haue all, sir, that may make
your *Hymen* high, and happy' (III. v. 49–52). These 'open
pleasures' reach their climax in III. vi and III. vii. The
nature and significance of this revelry is best understood in

---

[1] The traditions of riot and misrule which were associated with such
festive days are referred to by Jonson in *Time Vindicated to Himself and to His
Honours*, 253–7 (where they are associated with the traditions of the Saturnalia), and in *Bartholomew Fair*, v. i. 10.

relation to certain festive and wedding customs common in Jonson's time; it is in the light of these we must now examine these central scenes.

III

That Jonson was interested in such customs may be inferred from his own detailed notes to his Twelfth Night wedding masque of 1606, *Hymenaei* (written for the marriage of the daughter of the Earl of Suffolk, Frances Howard, with the Earl of Essex), where he drew on a variety of classical sources to explain the origin and nature of Roman wedding customs, some of which survived into his own time; and again from *A Tale of a Tub* where he declared his authorities were:

> old Records
> Of antique Proverbs, drawne from Whitson-Lord's,
> And their Authorities, at Wakes and Ales,
> With countrey precedents, and old Wives Tales.
>   (*Prologue*, 7–10)

The celebrations in *Epicoene* begin as a kind of parody of a courtly wedding masque, such as *Hymenaei*, and rapidly change into something else: the form of a popular ceremony used to deride ridiculous or irregular marriages.

Lady Haughty begins by asking—at Truewit's prompting —why this wedding is not being celebrated with all the traditional customs and 'markes of solemnitie': 'Wee see no ensignes of a wedding, here; no character of a brideale; where be our skarfes, and our gloues? I pray you, giue 'hem vs. Let's know your brides colours, and yours, at least' (III. vi. 70–3). Lady Haughty is asking, in short, for the wedding to be celebrated in the courtly style; Jonson himself had written three years earlier an epithalamion and a masque for Frances Howard's marriage; in his masque for her remarriage in 1614, *A Challenge at Tilt*, he was to introduce the device of the married couple's colours. But this travesty marriage can have only a travesty epithalamion (promised by Sir John Daw) and a travesty masque; a kind of wild antimasque, now led in by Clerimont:

> *Clerimont.* By your leaue, ladies. Doe you want any musique? I haue brought you varietie of noyses. Play, sirs, all of you.
>
> *Morose.* O, a plot, a plot, a plot, a plot vpon me! This day, I shall be their anvile to worke on, they will grate me asunder. 'Tis worse than the noyse of a saw.
>
> *Musique of all sorts.*
>
> *Clerimont.* No, they are haire, rosin, and guts. I can giue you the receipt.
>
> *Truewit.* Peace, boyes.
>
> *Clerimont.* Play, I say.
>
> *Truewit.* Peace, rascalls. You see who's your friend now sir? Take courage, put on a martyrs resolution. Mocke downe all their attemptings, with patience. 'Tis but a day, and I would suffer heroically.　　　　　　　　　　　　　　　　　(III. vii. 1–13)

Jonson has engineered the events of this and preceding scenes brilliantly to this climax (lost in Colman's later rearrangement); it is a climax beyond language, producing —like the explosion in Act IV of *The Alchemist*—sheer noise. 'Noyse' is a term for a band of musicians (Tobie Turfe in *A Tale of a Tub* commands 'all noises of *Finsbury*, in our name' to celebrate his daughter's wedding (I. iv. 50–1)), but the word reverts here to its general meaning as well: 'varietie of noyses' is made as Clerimont's musicians strike up discordantly and independently to produce '*Musique of all sorts*', against which the short quarrel of Clerimont and Truewit proceeds. The incident quite obviously carries symbolic implications; and to understand those implications one is tempted by the general masque-like atmosphere of this part of the play to a comparison with Jonson's use of

discordant music in his masques,[1] in particular with the
'*kind of contentious Musique*' raised in the early part of
Hymenaei by the four Humours and four Affections which
threaten to disturb the ceremonies. These, Jonson explains,
'were *tropically* brought in, before *Marriage*, as disturbers of
that *mysticall bodie*, and the *rites*, which were *soule* vnto it;
that afterwards, in *Marriage*, being dutifully tempered by
her *power*, they might more fully celebrate the happiness
of such as liue in that sweet *union*, to the harmonious lawes
of Nature and Reason' (Note on l. 112). And in *Hymenaei*
this discordant music gives way to 'sacred concords',
concords which, of course, never enter the jarring and
disunited world of *Epicoene*.

The symbolic nature of the incident in *Epicoene* under
discussion would not, I think, have been lost on an un-
learned audience at Whitefriars. For the ceremony to which
Morose is subjected is also very similar, both in its form
and its occasion, to certain festive ceremonies which that
audience almost certainly would have known. That which
it most resembles is the *charivari* or *chevauchée*, described as
follows by Cotgrave in his Dictionary of 1632: 'A public
defamation, or traducing of; a foule noise made, blacke
Santus rung, to the shame, and disgrace of another; hence,
an infamous (or infaming) ballade sung, by an armed troup,
under the window of an old dotard married, the day before,
unto a young wanton, in mockery of them both.' The
'foule noise' in question was usually made by the beating
of kettles, marrow-bones, and cleavers. E. K. Chambers
explains the various 'offences' which could be punished by

---

[1] *Love Freed from Ignorance and Folly*, 2; *The Masque of Queens*, 29–36;
Time Vindicated, 220, etc. Crites in *Cynthia's Revels* (v. v. 11–12) likens the
courtiers to 'a sort of jarring instruments, / All out of tune'. The symbolism
of marital discord appears again in the introductory description of the
uxorious Deliro in *Every Man Out of His Humour*, who wakes his wife every
morning with 'villainous-out-of-tune-music'.

this ceremony: 'A miser, a henpecked husband or a wife-
beater, especially in May, and on the other hand, a shrew
or an unchaste woman, are liable to visitation, as are the
parties to a second or third marriage, or to one perilously
long delayed, or one linking May to December.'[1] There was
a similar kind of musical cacophony in the related ceremony
of the skimmington, in which the victims, often represented
by neighbours or by effigies, were tied back-to-back on a
horse and accompanied through the streets by a crowd
of revellers playing discordantly on musical instruments.[2]
The primary purpose of such ceremonies as the *charivari*
and the skimmington was to punish through ridicule what
was thought to be the absurdest of marital aberrations, the
dominance of the wife:

> When wives their sexes shift, like hares
> And ride their husbands, like night-mares . . .
> (*Hudibras*, ii. ii. 705–6)

The *charivari*-like scene in *Epicoene* in fact celebrates (though
all the celebrants are not aware of the fact) the larger theme
of sexual reversal in the play, so well discussed by Edward

[1] E. K. Chambers, *The Mediaeval Stage* (Oxford 1903), i. 154. See also
Claude Noirot's account of the *charivari* in 'L'Origine des masques' (C. Leber,
Collection des Meilleurs Dissertations, Notices, et Traités (Paris, 1938), ix). A
somewhat similar ceremony is introduced in i. iii of *The English-Moor, or the
Mock Marriage*, by Jonson's follower Richard Brome. Its purpose is to deride
Quicksands, 'an old Usurer' newly married to a young wife. In 'The "Impure
Art" of John Webster', *R.E.S.*, n.s. ix (1958), pp. 253–67, Inga-Stina Ekeblad
argues that a *charivari* is introduced also by Webster in *The Duchess of Malfi*,
iv. ii. See also William Empson's discussion of the significance of such
ceremonies in *Some Versions of Pastoral* (2nd imp., London, 1950), pp. 51–2.

[2] The skimmington is described in detail by Samuel Butler in *Hudibras*,
Part ii, Canto ii, 565 ff., and is vividly brought alive in Hogarth's illustration
of this passage. (Another illustration of the skimmington, apparently based
on Hogarth's, may be found in the 1729 edition of Essex Hawker's play *The
Wedding*.) It still existed in certain parts of England at the time Hardy des-
cribed it in *The Mayor of Casterbridge*, Ch. 39. (See P. H. Ditchfield, *Old
English Customs* (London, 1896), pp. 178–81; Ruth A. Firor, *Folkways in
Thomas Hardy* (Philadelphia, 1931).)

Partridge in *The Broken Compass* (London, 1958), and as
such has application not just to Morose and Epicoene, but
also to the Otters and to the Collegiates. The wider purpose
of such ceremonies as the *charivari* seems to have been to
punish social eccentricity in its different manifestations:
miserliness, misanthropy, refusal to join in holiday revelry
(the ceremonies took place on holidays or on the days
immediately surrounding a wedding). Morose, being a miser,
a misanthrope, an enemy of holiday revelry, and 'an old
dotard married [it seems] unto a young wanton' is a natural
victim for such a visitation. His punishment, like the different punishment of Pinnacia Stuffe, the tailor's wife in
The New Inn, can only be fully understood by reference to
the traditions of contemporary festive customs. That such
traditions were found obscure even in the eighteenth century
is evident from Thomas Davies's comments upon the play's
revival in 1752: '. . . the frequent allusions to forgotten customs and characters render it impossible to be ever revived
with any probability of success. To understand Jonson's
comedies perfectly, we should have before us a satirical
history of the age in which he lived.'[1]

At many points *Epicoene* reminds one of *The Merchant of
Venice*; to Shylock music is 'vile squealing' and 'shallow

---

[1] *Dramatic Miscellanies* (London, 1784), ii. 101–2. If the specific allusions
of the play were not always understood in the eighteenth century, its general
significance seems to have been clear to Hogarth, whose drawing 'The
Enraged Musician' may have been partly inspired by the scene just discussed.
Castrucci, the leading violinist of the Italian opera, stands at the window of
his house, his hands to his ears as he is tormented by a variety of street noises:
a milkmaid and two tradesmen crying their wares, a boy beating a French
drum, a girl twirling her rattle, a postman sounding his horn, a parrot screech-
ing, a dog howling as its leg is broken by a grinder's wheel, and a pair of
cats noisily mating on a distant roof-top. Both Jonson's play and Hogarth's
picture represent an absurd attempt to live a secluded and exclusive life, an
attempt which is defeated by the invasion of the noises of common life.
George Colman's play of 1789, *Ut Pictura Poesis: or, The Enraged Musician*,
based both on *Epicoene* and on this drawing, confirms the impression that the
two were popularly associated.

fopp'ry' (II. v. 30, 35), as to Morose discourse itself is
'harsh, impertinent, and irksome' (II. i. 5); Shylock shuts
his casements against the sounds of revelry as Morose tries
to bar his doors against the wedding guests. That discourse,
music, and revelry are the things that traditionally draw
men together needs no pointing out; but what is conspicu-
ously absent in *Epicoene* is any equivalent to the Belmont
scenes in *The Merchant of Venice*, any equivalent to the
'concord of sweet sounds' of which Lorenzo speaks (v. i. 84),
or of the 'sacred concords' which come in *Hymenaei* as
masque replaces antimasque. The play ends not as comedy
traditionally does, in marriage, but in divorce. It is notable
that when in *The Old Bachelor* Congreve takes over this idea
of a fifth act 'divorce'—and the verbal echoes of *Epicoene*
are clear as Heartwell cries for a release from Silvia—he
removes the powerful Jonsonian feeling of continuing
disharmony and isolation by allowing the play to close with
the conventional promises of marriage; Bellmour will
marry Belinda, and Vainlove, Araminta. Jonson's ending
is uncompromising and harsh. George Colman in his
adaptation of the play in 1776 apparently wanted, like
Congreve, to temper this harshness when he cut Dauphine's
last stinging sentence to his uncle: 'Now you may goe in
and rest, and be as priuate as you will, sir. I'll not trouble
you, till you trouble me with your funerall, which I care
not how soone it come' (v. iv. 214–17). 'Privacy' could
not be more contemptuously restored. Morose may now
look forward to the ultimate and only privacy that can be
obtained, that of the grave; after his 'wedding', his funeral
will be the next and only occasion to draw people together
again on his behalf. The final isolation of Morose may bring
to mind the words of Sir John Daw's madrigal (II. iii. 29–30):

> *No noble vertue ever was alone,*
> *But two in one—*

words which seem to echo those which Jonson gave to 'Truth' in the Barriers of *Hymenaei*:

> Know then, the first *production* of things
> Required *two*, from mere *one* nothing springs . . .
>
> (724–5)

What the revelry of the play 'celebrates', indeed, is a complex and pervasive notion of isolation and disunity, the opposite qualities to those which wedding revelry should celebrate; to those qualities, in fact, celebrated in *Hymenaei*. As D. J. Gordon's excellent study of that masque shows,[1] *Hymenaei* celebrates the perfect union of soul and body and of their humours and affections; of individual and individual, family and family, kingdom and kingdom, and of the divine plan itself. Private and public virtues are celebrated together, because private and public worlds are seen to be in perfect harmony with each other. Outward emblems—the 'show' of the masque, the colours and costumes of the masquers, the very bodies of the married couple—are perfect indexes of inward grace in the spirit of the masque and the masquers. 'Peace' extends outwards from the marriage of two individuals to that of their families and of the different parts of the kingdom, and to King James's peaceful policy abroad; a peace likened to that of Christ himself.[2] In *Epicoene* there is no such harmonious union between public and private worlds, between outward appearance and inward truth, between individual

---

[1] '*Hymenaei*: Ben Jonson's Masque of Union', *Journal of the Warburg and Courtauld Institutes*, viii (1945), pp. 107–45.

[2] The actual outcome of the marriage celebrated in this masque was, of course, less happy. Gifford was in fact reminded by the 'divorce' scene of *Epicoene* of the real-life divorce of Essex: 'If it were not ascertained beyond a doubt that the *Silent Woman* appeared on the stage in 1609, four years at least prior to the date of that most infamous transaction, it would be difficult to persuade the reader that a strong burlesque of it was not here intended.' *The Works of Ben Jonson*, ed. W. Gifford (London, 1816), iii. 485–6.

and individual; instead of peace, there is 'strife and tumult', 'disease', and isolation.

Comparison of the themes of stage play and masque suggests, finally, the possibility of comparing the nature of the decorum which controls and gives unity to each work. The 'matter' of Jonson's Court masques is normally appropriate to the special nature of the festive days upon which they were presented, as we have in part already seen—Christmas, Twelfth Night, Shrovetide, May Day, etc. As I suggested in the last chapter, this kind of occasional appropriateness in not confined to the masques. *Cynthia's Revels*, for instance, designed for presentation at Court on Twelfth Night, 1601, takes an occasion of Court revels as its theme; its appropriateness to the day it celebrates is as obvious as that of, say, *Time Vindicated to Himself and to His Honours*. As Jonson's stage plays, unlike his masques, were intended for repeated performance, such exact occasional appropriateness as that in *Cynthia's Revels* or, say *Christmas His Masque* was not always possible. But it seems not without significance that the action of several of Jonson's avowedly 'popular' plays takes place upon a holiday, and is appropriate to the holiday spirit. This is true, for instance, of *Bartholomew Fair*, *The New Inn*, and *A Tale of a Tub*, as well as of *Epicoene*. The popular, festive aim of *Epicoene* is acknowledged (not without irony) by Jonson in the Prologue:

> Our wishes, like to those make publique feasts
> Are not to please the cookes taste, but the guests. (8–9)

The play is festive in mood, and depicts a festive occasion; a quarter-day feast merging with a wedding. In her treatment of Morose, Epicoene seems to be claiming both the traditional liberties of a bride upon her wedding-day, and the traditional holiday liberties of which Pan speaks in Jonson's May Day *Entertainment at Highgate*:

The yong Nymph, that's troubled with an old man,
Let her laugh him away, as fast as she can.   (239–40)

A similar wedding 'licence' (to use Jonson's own pun) falls unexpectedly to Grace Wellborn in *Bartholomew Fair*, the occasion of which is both her wedding-day and a holiday, St. Bartholomew's Day; Awdrey Turfe in *A Tale of a Tub* enjoys similar freedoms on her St. Valentine's Day wedding-day, when—in Tobie Turfe's phrase—'All things run *Arsie-Varsie*; upside downe' (III. i. 2). In each of these plays, as in *The New Inn*, the action seems to be confined to one day, not simply because this was what the classical laws required, but because one day was also the duration of the 'laws' of holiday. Hence Dryden's observation about Jonson's 'making choice' in *Epicoene* 'of some signal and long-expected day, whereon the action of the play is to depend'[1] begins to take on an additional significance. At the end of this 'signal and long-expected day' Morose's torments will be over, and he may live as 'priuate' as he pleases:

Take patience, good vncle. This is but a day, and 'tis well worne too now.   (IV. iv. 19–21)

Take courage, put on a martyrs resolution. Mocke downe all their attemptings, with patience. 'Tis but a day, and I would suffer heroically.   (III. vii. 11–13)

[1] *Essays*, ed. cit. i. 87.

CHAPTER THREE

'Days of Privilege': *Bartholomew Fair*

> Methinks the Days of *Bartholomew-Fair* are like so many
> Sabbaths, or Days of Privilege, wherein Criminals and
> Malefactors in Poetry, are permitted to creep abroad.
> They put me in mind (tho' at a different time of Year) of
> the Roman *Saturnalia*, when all the Scum, and Rabble, and
> Slaves of Rome, by a kind of annual and limited Manu-
> mission, were suffered to make abominable Mirth, and
> profane the Days of *Jubilee*, with vile Buffoonry, by
> Authority.
>
> CONGREVE to DENNIS, 11 August 1695.[1]

I

IT is sometimes said that in *Bartholomew Fair* Jonson seems
to relax the full seriousness and formal control that he had
shown in his earlier major comedies, *Volpone* and *The
Alchemist*, and that the play belongs to a lower, altogether
less serious order of comedy. L. C. Knights, for instance,
in an influential essay on Jonson, relegates the play along
with *Epicoene* to 'the category of stage entertainments' in
which 'the fun is divorced from any rich significance'.[2]
Yet there are some oddities about this view of the play as
a simple and amiable piece of theatrical fun. Perhaps the
first thing one notices about *Bartholomew Fair* is its length
and intricacy, the manner in which events crowd in with
something of the organized congestion of, say, *The Way of
the World*, demanding an intellectual attentiveness different
in kind from that usually exacted by the simpler kinds of
comedy. The narrative complexity of *Bartholomew Fair*

---

[1] *The Complete Works of William Congreve*, ed. M. Summers (London, 1923),
i. 95–6.
[2] L. C. Knights, 'Ben Jonson, Dramatist', in *The Age of Shakespeare*, Vol. 2
of *A Guide to English Literature*, ed. Boris Ford (London, 1955), pp. 302–17.

is matched by a complexity of tone. Like *Epicoene*, *Bartholomew Fair* is often described as a genial play, in which Jonson's accustomed harshness gives way to a new moral and theatrical humility.[1] In some obvious ways this description is true; yet it is impossible to miss the irony and hostility behind Jonson's apparently concessive remarks in the Induction that the play is written just to the '*Meridian*' of the Stage-Keeper and of 'the vnderstanding Gentlemen o' the ground' (56, 49); such gentlemen had damned *Catiline* three years earlier, and were 'understanding' only in the sense that they stood in the pit. Jonson seems now to acknowledge the fact that 'the Drama's Laws the Drama's Patrons give', and to propose a new play written to these laws; yet at the same time he allows us to sense his contempt for such popular tyranny, and his higher valuation of other dramatic laws:

> If there bee neuer a *Seruant-monster* i' the *Fayre*; who can helpe it? he sayes; nor a nest of *Antiques*? Hee is loth to make Nature afraid in his *Playes*, like those that beget *Tales*, *Tempests*, and such like *Drolleries*, to mixe his head with other mens heeles, let the concupisence of *Iigges* and *Dances*, raigne as strong as it will amongst you: yet if the *Puppets* will please any body, they shall be entreated to come in.   (127–34)

The criticism of Shakespeare's use of romance convention, though seriously made, is curiously neutralized as Jonson shifts his ground with deliberate absurdity: the playwright who is loth to make nature afraid now professes himself equally loth to displease his paying audience (perhaps it is no accident that the puppets are later referred to as 'monsters': III i. 12, v. iv. 28). Mixing 'his head with other mens heeles' is exactly what Jonson himself will do in *Bartholomew Fair*; this classic image of reversed order ('Let's

---

[1] See, for example, Jonas Barish's fine discussion of the play in his *Ben Jonson and the Language of Prose Comedy* (Cambridge, Mass., 1960), Ch. v.

have the giddy world turn'd the heeles upward')[1] is allowed
to infiltrate with a delicate appropriateness. The criticism
which Jonson levelled at Shakespeare may now be levelled
at him, for each playwright is complying with the tyranny
of popular dramatic taste; as so often in the play, the judge
turns out to be an offender himself. The wry, somewhat
angry paradox is delineated with some sophistication. Such
sophistication is of quite a different order from the 'noise'
and 'sport' which the Scrivener promises to the groundlings,
and helps to encourage at this early stage an awareness that
the comedy is appealing simultaneously at two different
levels. This awareness persists throughout the play itself; and
we cannot help but remember Jonson's implications about
the literary taste of his age as we hear Littlewit, Overdo,
Leatherhead, and Busy discourse in their different ways
about the vanity of learning, of poetry, and of the stage itself.

     While observing the double-level appeal that the play
has—robust, noisy farce, overlaid by cool, ironic reflection upon the implications of such entertainment—we
may recall that, historically speaking, *Bartholomew Fair* had
two audiences. So far as we know, it was performed only
twice in Jonson's lifetime: once on Hallow E'en, 1614,
at the Hope Theatre, and again the very next day, All
Saints' Day, at Court.[2] Jonson dedicated the play to King
James, and addressed to him too the special prologue and
epilogue written for Court performance. In several senses
of the term, *Bartholomew Fair* is an occasional play: it is

---

[1] *Time Vindicated*, 219. In *Hymenaei* Jonson spoke of the perfect blending
of the device of the author and the execution of the dancers: the dance
'seemed to take away that *Spirit* from the Inuention, which the *Inuention*
gaue to it: and left it doubtfull, whether the Formes flow'd more perfectly
from the Author's braine, or their feete'.

[2] Herford and Simpson, *Ben Jonson*, ed. cit. ix. 245. The Dedication to James
appears on the title-page of the 1640 Folio (set up in type for printing in
1631): 'Acted in the Yeare, 1614. By the Lady Elizabeth's Servants. And then
dedicated to King James, of most Blessed Memorie. . . .'

designed for performance upon two particular holiday occasions, and it takes for its theme the events of another particular holiday occasion, St. Bartholomew's Day. With the skill of an experienced masque-writer, Jonson relates the occasion inside the play to the occasions which frame it. The performance of the play before King James would seem to have a significance of particular interest which has hitherto gone unnoticed; we may leave the unravelling of this to a later part of this chapter, and turn first to the Induction of the play, which recreates the sense of its first public performance.

The play is still mistakenly praised for its classical single-ness of time and place;[1] yet in this respect (as in other respects) the play's real effect is one of multiplicity. Two dates are actually named: in the Induction, the Articles of Agreement with the audience are dated 31 October, the actual day of performance; the action of the play itself takes place on 24 August, as Littlewit points out with delighted care in the opening moments of the play's first scene: 'to day! the foure and twentieth of August! *Bartholmew* day! *Bartholmew* vpon *Bartholmew*! there's the deuice!' It is the device,[2] as we shall see, upon which the whole play turns. There are also two locations (quite apart from Littlewit's house, where the first act takes place): the Hope Theatre and Smithfield. By way of an apparent apology for a trifling technical flaw, Jonson draws the two locations together in our minds: 'And though the *Fayre* be not kept in the same Region, that some here, perhaps, would haue it, yet thinke, that therein the *Author* hath obseru'd a speciall *Decorum*, the place being as durty as *Smithfield*, and as stinking euery whit' (156–60). To interpret this 'speciall *Decorum*' as

[1] e.g. *Bartholomew Fair*, ed. Eugene M. Waith, *The Yale Ben Jonson* (New Haven and London, 1963), Introduction, p. 20.

[2] The common term for the contrivance of a dramatic piece (*O.E.D.* 9). At III. iv. 162 Cokes plans the 'deuice' of his own wedding masque.

evidence for Jonson's respect for the classical rules would seem unnecessarily obtuse. The audience is invited to pass judgement on the action they are about to see; it is subtly suggested that in doing so they will be passing judgement on themselves.

Smithfield traditionally enjoyed, for the duration of its annual Fair, what were known as its 'Liberties and Privileges'.[1] In the Induction to the play, Jonson grants to the audience at the Hope Theatre comparable liberties and privileges, in the form of the Articles of Agreement. The word which most powerfully conveys Jonson's complex feelings about such liberties is the word *licence*, which operates throughout the play as a kind of unifying pun.[2] A licence may be either a right that is freely granted, or a right that is freely (and wrongfully) taken. The drawing-up of a form of licence with the audience setting out the terms in which they may criticize the play serves to throw attention on the traditional licence, or freedom, with which they are accustomed to judge the plays they see. Jonson later returns to this idea in *The Magnetic Lady*, where Damplay insists upon his rights to censure the play that he is watching:

> I care not for marking the *Play*: Ile damne it, talke, and doe that I come for. I will not have *Gentlemen* lose their priviledge, nor I my selfe my prerogative, for neere an overgrowne, or superannuated Poët of 'hem all. He shall not give me the Law; I will censure, and be witty, and take my Tobacco, and enjoy my *Magna Charta* of reprehension, as my Predecessors have done before me.
> *Boy.* Even to license, and absurdity.
>
> (*Chorus* before Act IV, 19–25)

---

[1] Cornelius Walford, *Fairs, Past and Present* (London, 1883), p. 205.

[2] Ray L. Heffner, jun., in an essay to which the present study is obviously indebted, sees the play as centring on the notion of 'warrant': 'Unifying Symbols in the Comedy of Ben Jonson', in *English Stage Comedy* (*English Institute Essays*), ed. W. K. Wimsatt, jun. (New York, 1954), pp. 74–97. I am grateful to Mr. Emrys Jones for first drawing my attention to the importance of 'licence' in this play.

And in *The Staple of News* the censorious gossips abrogate to themselves a similar licence as they watch and criticize the action of the play. Gossip Mirth declares herself to be '*the daughter of* Christmas, *and spirit of* Shrouetide' (Induction, 11–12); the allusion—and it is a relevant one to the understanding of *Bartholomew Fair*—is to the licence traditionally connected with holiday revelry.

Like *Epicoene*, *Bartholomew Fair* is best regarded as a festive comedy. The feeling of Saturnalia is abroad as early as the Induction, where the groundlings are formally set up as judges for a limited period of 'two houres and an halfe, and somewhat more' (the '*Bench*' on which they sit is that of the magistrate's court as well as that of the Hope Theatre), where their Articles of Agreement are signed 'preposterously' (back-to-front, by their having paid their money before they have heard the terms read), and where a Stage-Keeper passes confident judgement against the practice of 'these Master-*Poets*' who have 'their owne absurd courses' (79–80, 104, 153, 26–7). Such freedoms and inversions may remind us of those in the antimasque of *Time Vindicated*, where Ears, Eyes, and Nose speak with relish of those 'dayes of feast, and libertie', 'where men might doe, and talke all that they list', planning to turn 'all things out of order' (43, 44, 221). Within the play itself, the occasion for such freedoms is multiple: it is St. Bartholomew's Day, it is the day of Bartholomew Cokes's wedding to Grace Wellborn (which Cokes wishes to celebrate with 'a fine young masque', III. iv. 93), and it is also, as in *The Staple of News*, the day which marks the final liberation of a ward from his tutor: Cokes from Wasp (and, we might add, Grace from her guardian Overdo).

The play's first act introduces us to three figures who enjoy the exercise of different, minor kinds of authority: Littlewit, the proctor, or attorney, at the ecclesiastical Court of the Arches; Humphrey Wasp, the 'governor', or tutor, of Cokes; and Zeal-of-the-Land Busy, the Puritan elder. Later, Justice Adam Overdo will join their number. The comedy tests, in turn, the authority of each man, and finds it wanting. Power, authority, and intelligence lie in this play not with the masters but with the servants (the point is made in the very names: Master Littlewit has a servant called Solomon) and with the sharpers who stand watching on the side-lines. As the movement of the comedy becomes more intricate it becomes evident that even these men depend upon the luck of the game, that the events which occur at Smithfield Fair are not subject to human control.

Proctor Littlewit, though a man of the law, is himself lawless, his lawlessness showing itself in his talk, which eddies away constantly in wildly turning conceits. '*A wise tongue* should not be licentious, and wandering,' Jonson declared in *Discoveries*, 'but mov'd, and (as it were) govern'd with certain raines from the heart, and bottome of the brest . . .' (330–3). The sprawling, 'ungovern'd' talk of Littlewit gives an immediate indication of his character, just as the different kinds of nonsensically-proliferating language of Wasp, Overdo, and Busy (sensitively analysed by Jonas Barish) alert us at once to the lack of authority of these men. The first subject, indeed, to which Littlewit exuberantly turns is that of his own habits of speech: 'When a quirk, or a *quiblin* do's scape thee, and thou dost not watch, and apprehend it, and bring it afore the Constable of conceit: (there now, I speake *quib* too) let 'hem carry thee out o' the Archdeacons Court, into his Kitchin, and make a *Iack* of thee, in stead of a *Iohn*. (There I am againe la!)' (I. i. 13–18). Such an exotic disquisition on the subject of control—intellectual, as well as legal, for to 'apprehend' (Littlewit's favourite word) is to understand as well as to arrest—suggests its opposite, licence.

Later in the scene, Littlewit throws up another fantas-
ticated legal metaphor: 'But gi' mee the man, can start
vp a *Iustice* of *Wit* out of six-shillings beare, and giue the
law to all the *Poets*, and *Poet-suckers* i' Towne, because they
are the Players Gossips' (I. i. 38–41). Jonson has
here circled back—as he does so often throughout the
play—to the theme of the Induction: authority and judgement in literary matters. Littlewit is an amateur poet, who
has written a puppet-play for performance in the Fair. His
metaphor (' a *Iustice* of *Wit*') invites us to see authority in
literary matters as analogous to authority in legal matters;
the basis of such authority is nothing but the stimulus of
small beer, which can prompt Littlewit to 'giue the law'
to the other poets of the town. Jonson ironically contrasts
his own position as a dramatist with that of Littlewit:
Jonson himself is amongst those poets lorded over by
Littlewit and his fellow Smithfield poets (just as he is one of
those 'Master-*Poets*' lorded over by the Stage-Keeper). We
are in the world of Pope's *Dunciad*.

The two other governors enjoy an equally absurd and
precarious authority. Zeal-of-Land Busy is 'one, that, they
say, is come heere, and gouernes all, already' (I. iii. 106–7).
This 'old Elder' turns out (in one of the easy, punning
reversals of the play) to be no more than a child: 'by his
profession, hee will euer be i' the State of Innocence,
though; and child-hood; derides all *Antiquity*; defies any
other *Learning*, then *Inspiration*; and what discretion soeuer,
yeeres should afford him, it is all preuented in his *Originall
ignorance* ...'. Humphrey Wasp, 'governor' to Bartholomew
Cokes, is soon to display a comparable childishness. Later
in the play he is indeed to carry Cokes about the Fair on his
back, as Aeneas carried his aged father Anchises;[1] but here,

---

[1] *Aeneid* ii. 721 ff. Aeneas' carrying of Anchises out of Troy was commonly adduced in Renaissance emblem books to illustrate the virtue of filial

absurdly, the older man carries the younger. Always un-
controllable in temperament, Wasp at his first appearance
turns instantly (like Littlewit) to the question of control:

> *Wasp.* Why, say I haue a humour not to be ciuill; how then?
> who shall compell me? you? . . . I haue a charge. Gentlemen.
> *Littlewit.* They doe apprehend, Sir.
> *Wasp.* Pardon me, Sir, neither they nor you, can apprehend mee,
> yet. (you are an Asse).   (I. iv. 60–70)

Wasp trumps Littlewit with his own pun; Littlewit can
neither *understand* nor *restrain* the irascible tutor.

Cokes has been left in the temporary charge of his sister,
Mistress Overdo; 'But what may happen, vnder a womans
gouernment,' says Wasp darkly, 'there's the doubt.' And
when Mistress Overdo appears with her charge in I. v,
Wasp bustles in to recover control: 'you thinke, you are
Madam *Regent* still, Mistris *Ouer-doo*; when I am in place?
no such matter, I assure you, your *raigne* is out, when I am
in, *Dame*.' 'Madam *Regent*' may remind us of the shrewish
world of *Epicoene* ('She is my Regent already', says Morose
after his wedding to the Epicoene); and the whole formula
is recalled in an illuminating way in *The New Inn*. In this
play a chambermaid, Prue, has been elected a temporary
'Queen of the day's sports' which take place at the inn;
at the end of the day, she is forced to relinquish her role:

> Your raigne is ended, *Pru*, no soueraigne now:
> Your date is out, and dignity expir'd.
>   (v. iv. 16–17)

piety: see *Andreae Alciati Emblematum Libellus* (Paris, 1534), p. 73; Geoffrey
Whitney, *A Choice of Emblemes* (Leyden, 1586), p. 163. Jonson is here probably burlesquing this well-known figure. In *The New Inn*, I. vi. 133–7, he
alludes more directly to the Anchises incident, this time to describe an
exemplary relationship between a young man and an old. (An almost
identical pick-a-back scene frequently illustrates *mutuum auxilium* in the
emblem books: Alciati, op. cit., p. 26, Whitney, op. cit., p. 65; and cf. the
discussion of *mutua auxilia* in Jonson's *Discoveries*, 65–73.)

Mistress Overdo's role, too, Wasp implies, is as temporary as that of a holiday queen; yet by the end of the play his rule, too, will be as easily overthrown:

Cokes. Hold your peace, Numpes; you ha' beene i' the Stocks, I heare.
Wasp. Do's he know that? nay, then the date of my *Authority* is out; I must thinke no longer to raigne, my gouerment is at an end. He that will correct another, must want fault in himselfe.

(v. iv. 95–100)

He that will correct another, must want fault in himselfe: here we are at the heart of the comedy; the farcical, festive reversals are allowed to carry profounder, Christian implications. As Mistress Overdo says to Wasp in the first act, 'I am content to be in *abeyance*, Sir, and be gouern'd by you; so should hee too, if he did well; but 'twill be expected, you should also gouerne your passions.' This idea that the governor must first learn to govern himself is played over in a rich variety of ways throughout the play; later we shall investigate its special appropriateness at the Court performance of the play. In the third act (scene v, 288–90) Grace makes a similar remark about her guardians:

Winwife. You see what care they haue on you, to leaue you thus.
Grace. Faith, the same they haue of themselues, Sir.

In the words of the old song, 'Who takes care of the caretaker's daughter while the caretaker's busy taking care?' And, more searchingly, *quis custodiet custodes?* It is upon such questions that the comedy turns.

Or again, the subject of the play might be seen as that of *discipline*. 'Now, the blaze of the beauteous discipline, fright away this euill from our house!', says Dame Purecraft (I. vi. 1–2), using a cherished Puritan phrase; Tribulation Wholesome in *The Alchemist* (III. i. 32) also speaks of his faith's 'beauteous discipline'. Jonson's use of the word

'discipline' in a dramatic context is almost always ironical:
'I will haue this order reverst,' says Moria in *Cynthia's
Revels*, 'there must be a reform'd discipline', and we know
that her only discipline lies in the consistent practice of
folly; Face in *The Alchemist* declares the triumvirate 'safe,
by their discipline, against a world', and we know at once
how fragile and vulnerable that alliance is. Dame Purecraft's
'discipline', likewise, is the reverse of discipline, as the
veering course of her actions is soon to show (her name
means 'sheer cunning' as well as 'chaste strength'). In
the fifth act Quarlous, disguised as the madman Trouble-all,
is to speak the truth: 'Away, you are a heard of hypocriticall
proud Ignorants, rather wilde, then mad. Fitter for woods,
and the society of beasts then houses, and the congregation
of men. You are the second part of the society of *Canters*,
Outlawes to order and *Discipline* . . .' (v. ii. 41–5).

Zeal-of-the-Land Busy, summoned at the end of the
first act to declare his opinion whether or not Fair-going
'can be any way made, or found lawfull', gives us yet
another variant of mock-discipline; rigidly opposed (like
Morose) to '*Fayres* and *May-games*, *Wakes*, and *Whitson-ales*',
Busy nevertheless zig-zags piously and pedantically towards
the inevitable conclusion: they will all go to the Fair:

> Now Pigge, it is a meat, and a meat that is nourishing, and may
> be long'd for, and so consequently eaten; it may be eaten; very
> exceeding well eaten; but in the *Fayre*, and as a *Bartholmew*-pig,
> it cannot be eaten, for the very calling it a *Bartholmew*-pigge,
> and to eat it so, is a spice of *Idolatry*, and you make the *Fayre*,
> no better then one of the high *Places*. This I take it, is the state
> of the question. A high place.   (I. vi. 50–7)

'No better then one of the high *Places*' is good; the apocalyptic Old Testament texts which Busy's words suggest
('exalt him that is low, and abase him that is high', for
instance: Ezekiel 21:26) also suggest nicely the kind of

reversals which the comedy, too, will bring about. Littlewit's quip reinforces the suggestion: 'I, but in a state of necessity: *Place* should giue place, Mr. *Busy*, (I haue a conceit left, yet.)' '*Place* should giue place': Littlewit's phrase is, in its context, almost meaningless, yet it alerts us to the continual comic displacements which occur throughout the play: 'You thinke, you are Madam *Regent* still, Mistris *Ouer-doo*; when I am in place?' Like the cluster of words already noticed—free will, liberty, licence, reign, discipline, govern, apprehend—*place* reminds us of law and natural order. Trouble-all the madman is later revealed to have been 'an officer in the Court of *Pie-poulders*, here last yeere, and put out on his place by Iustice *Ouerdoo*' (IV. i. 54–5). Wasp, too, is finally 'put out on his place'. In the Induction to the play each member of the audience has covenanted that 'his place get not aboue his wit' (90–1). On festival days, says Joan Trash, Leatherhead the puppet-man must take his 'place' by right at the head of the table (III. iv. 124). As people are dislodged in turn from their places in the course of this play we may be reminded of Lear's phrase: 'Change places, and handy-dandy, which is the justice, which is the thief?' Roles are to be subjected to constant confusion, the high are to be brought low.

Lear's words, and those of Busy, are recalled at the beginning of the second act: Justice Adam Overdo is one who lives (so he says) 'in high place' (II. i. 36). So far from living in high place, Overdo is simply an occasional judge in the lowest court of the kingdom, the Court of Pie-Powders, which met for three days of the year 'for the redresse of all disorders' committed in the Fair.[1] The power possessed by a judge of the Court of Pie-Powders was, indeed, an

---

[1] *Bartholomew Fair*, ed. E. A. Horsman, The Revels Plays (Cambridge, Mass., 1960), Introduction, p. xx; *Minsheu*, 1617, quoted Herford and Simpson, ed. cit. x. 186.

absolute one—not even James himself could intrude upon the jurisdiction of this court—but severely limited in time and scope.[1] Overdo has chosen to use his brief period of judicial license to dress as a madman and to spy out the enormities of the Fair. 'They may haue seene many a foole in the habite of a Iustice; but neuer till now, a Iustice in the habit of a foole.' Lear's handy-dandy is brought into the world of comedy; Overdo is already fool enough in his own right, and this is a situation like that so dear to Elizabethan comedy where a boy plays a girl playing a boy: here a fool plays a judge playing a fool. Between playing a fool and being a fool (the point is made several times in the play) there may not be much to choose.

As in so many of Jonson's other plays, the dramatic excitement of *Bartholomew Fair* arises out of the constant uncertainty as to who is in charge, and who is tricking whom, as the cleverest of devices backfire upon their devisors. At the end of the second act Adam Overdo preaches against the evils of liquor and tobacco; Edgworth the cutpurse takes advantage of the diversion to pick Cokes's pocket. 'There is a doing of right out of wrong, if the way be found', Overdo has declared at his first appearance; not until later is he to realize 'what bad euents may peepe out o' the taile of good purposes!' (II. i. 11–12; III. iii. 13–14). His plan to curb crime simply assists crime to thrive. Meanwhile Cokes, finding his purse gone, places his second purse where the first was taken, declaring gleefully that he has set 'a delicate fine trap to catch the cutpurse, nibling' (II. vi. 131–2). The two 'traps' of Overdo and Cokes deliciously match each other: neither man realizes his trap will simply close upon himself. Overdo's trap springs first: Wasp accuses him of being 'the Patriarch of the cutpurses', and the act ends in noise and confusion:

[1] H. Morley, *Memoirs of Bartholomew Fair* (London, 1859), pp. 97, 149.

'*They speake all together: and* Waspe *beats the* Iustice.' Cokes's trap springs next, in III. v.

In this scene Edgworth and the ballad-singer Nightingale conspire to pick Cokes's second purse: the purse disappears as Cokes listens, entranced, to Nightingale's song: 'A caueat against cutpurses.' Cokes is constantly vexed by two problems: how to apply the lessons of art to real life, as here: listening to a song warning him of the dangers of having his purse stolen, he fails to realize it may have applicability to a real situation; and how to know where art ends and real life begins, as in the puppet-show in Act Five; like Busy, Cokes is confused by the nature of fiction ('Betweene you and I Sir', says Leatherhead confidingly to him, 'we doe but make show': v. iv. 279). All eyes, ears, and curiosity, Cokes fails in what Jonson calls *understanding*, the ability to ponder and interpret that which is presented ('I scarce vnderstand 'hem', he says of the puppets: v. iv. 145–6). The tag at the head of Jonson's masque *Loves Triumph Through Callipolis* (1630), 'To make the Spectators vnderstanders', indicates one of the dramatist's perennial concerns. In his inexhaustible curiosity and impervious ignorance Cokes resembles the audience at the Hope Theatre, those 'vnderstanding Gentlemen o' the ground' whom Jonson finds he must warn in the Induction against making too literal an equation of what they are about to see with real life ('to search out, who was meant by the *Gingerbread-woman* . . .' etc.) but who will finally lack the ability to discern that the follies presented in this comedy may be somewhat like their own. Failure to understand a play, it is implied, is a failure to understand life itself.

Behind this idea lies, of course, the metaphor of the world as a stage. Throughout *Bartholomew Fair* the characters often use a terminology which can only be described as theatrical, giving the curious effect of double-focus. 'Wee had wonderfull ill lucke, to misse this prologue o' the purse,' says Quarlous to Winwife in III. ii, 'but the best is, we shall haue fiue *Acts* of him ere night: hee'le be spectacle enough!' 'Fiue *Acts*': for the real audience there are only two and a half to go. And the puppet show at the end of *Bartholomew Fair* gives, as we shall see, a similar hall-of-mirrors effect. In III. ii Ursula the pig-woman speaks of the 'guests' who are coming 'to fill my pit' in the Fair (108–9): they are like the guests who have come to fill the pit of the Hope Theatre (the theatre in fact served as a bear-pit once a fortnight,[1] as Ursula's very name—'little bear'—may remind us). Such references as these continually suggest the resemblances between the world of the play and the world of real life.

Merging with this metaphor of the theatre is another, equally powerful one: that of life as a game. The constant use of gaming imagery deepens the notion that things are set at hazard, that they are no longer subject to rational control. The purse-cutting scene of II. v suggests a teaser rather like that of Montaigne playing with his cat: might not the cat rather be playing with him? Who's in charge? Nightingale and Edgworth are playing an elaborate game to catch Cokes; their game (unknown to them) is being quietly observed by Winwife and Quarlous, who remark upon it as 'sport' (and, as the ripples spread out, this is the 'sport' which Jonson has promised both to the groundlings and to King James);[2] Cokes meanwhile is playing a naïvely defiant counter-game against what he takes to be a purely hypothetical cut-purse:

> . . . looke here, here's for him; handy-dandy, which *Hee shewes*
> hand will he haue?   *his purse.*
>
>   (III. v. 116–17)

---

[1] Herford and Simpson, ed. cit. x. 174.
[2] Induction, 82; Prologue, 8.

'Handy-dandy'—we have met the phrase already—is a children's game, in which a small object is shaken between the hands of one of the players, both hands then being suddenly closed, and the other player asked to guess which hand contains the object. Cokes is evidently playing this game as he speaks this line, first showing the purse, then holding out two closed fists. As in *King Lear*, the mention of this game has wider reverberations; it enforces the feeling of haphazardness, of affairs not being ordered by logic or by natural superiority but by guesswork and chance. As in *King Lear*, judge and thief are levelled; Nightingale's song tells how the judges in Westminster Hall are as vulnerable as himself:

> *Then why should the Iudges be free from this curse,*
> *More then my poore self, for cutting a purse?*
>   (III. v. 89–90)

('This curse' carries two senses: pickpockets will stop at nothing, even judges find them a menace; judges as well as ordinary mortals are flesh and blood and carry the sin of Adam.) From the beginning of the play this feeling of arbitrariness has been suggested by the constant use of gamester's language. It is 'a leap-frogge chance', 'a very lesse than *Ames-ace* [double ace], on two Dice' (I. i. 9–10), that Bartholomew Cokes should happen to be married upon St. Bartholomew's Day (no possibility of his having *chosen* the day is even entertained); it is '*crosse* and *pile* [in effect, heads or tails] whether for a new farthing' Wasp is trying to say that his charge is a silly man, or a fine one (I. iv. 93–4); Cokes, the victim of Edgworth's 'sport call'd *Dorring the Dottrell*' in IV. ii, ruefully says he 'had bin better ha' gone to mum chance' (a dice game) than try to choose which man he can trust and which he cannot (21, 75); Overdo, too, finds himself playing a game which he can barely master: 'Here might I ha' beene deceiu'd now: and ha' put a fooles blot vpon my selfe, if I had not play'd an after game o' discretion' (II. iii. 40–2).

The game takes a new turn at the end of Act Three. Grace Wellborn suddenly finds herself alone, out of the protection of Overdo (her guardian), Mistress Overdo (his deputy for the day), Cokes (her husband-to-be), and Wasp (her husband-to-be's governor). Quarlous and Winwife each has designs upon her. Quarlous corners Edgworth, whose sleight of hand with Cokes's second purse he has just observed, and blackmails him into stealing the licence from Wasp's black box. The black box plays a central, symbolic, ambiguous function in *Bartholomew Fair*, just as another black box was later to do (as we shall see) in *The Way of the World*. Edgworth thinks that the box must contain some kind of certificate that endorses Wasp's governorship, and that Quarlous wants to usurp Wasp's place. Jonson allows his audience, too, to be mystified about Quarlous's intentions until well on into the fourth act: what Quarlous intends is to use Cokes's wedding licence in order to steal Cokes's bride.[1] *Licence*, indeed.

Grace has a good many similarities with another girl who is left to her own devices upon her holiday wedding-day, and who is pursued by several suitors: Awdrey Turfe in *A Tale of a Tub*. Grace at first appears to be all moderation and good sense, naturally reluctant to be married to the vacuous Cokes, even though she realizes it would be possible to 'gouerne him, and enioy a friend, beside' (IV. iii. 14–15). Yet Grace's common sense has its limits; like Awdrey, she is so anxious to be rid of one fool that she will willingly marry another without delay:

'Tis true, I haue profest it to you ingenuously, that rather then

---

[1] The device of stealing a marriage licence is repeated in *The Magnetic Lady*.

to be yoak'd with this Bridegroome is appointed me, I would
take vp any husband, almost vpon any trust.

> (*Bartholomew Fair*, IV. iii. 10–13)

> Husbands, they say, grow thick; but thin are sowne;
> I care not who it be, so I have one.
>> (*A Tale of a Tub*, III. vi. 43–4)

For all her talk of love and reason, Grace finally chooses a
husband irrationally, by means of a game as arbitrary as
handy-dandy, deciding to leave her choice to 'fate' or
'*Destiny*'.

> I smile to thinke how like a Lottery
> These Weddings are,

says Hugh in *A Tale of a Tub* (I. i. 97–8)—the general,
sententious nature of the saying being sharpened by the
St. Valentine's setting of the play, for on this day partners
were actually chosen by means of drawing lots.[1] Grace too
chooses herself a partner by an equally random method.
She makes her rival suitors, Quarlous and Winwife, write
on a 'paire of tables' 'a word, or a name, what you like
best': Quarlous chooses a name out of Sidney's *Arcadia*,
'Argalus', and Winwife one from *Two Noble Kinsmen*,
'Palamon'. Again, there is the odd feeling of real life
blending with fiction, and also of a kind of levelling: one
man is as good as another; Quarlous and Winwife are
reduced to Tweedledum and Tweedledee, as little differ-
entiated as Damon and Pythias in the puppet-play in Act
Five or the masked ladies who watch that play ('Giue me
twelue pence from tee, and dou shalt haue eder-oder on
'hem!': v. iv. 52–3). '. . . . you are both equall, and alike
to mee, yet:', says Grace to her two suitors, 'and so in-
differently affected by mee, as each of you might be the

---

[1] A. R. Wright, *British Calendar Customs*, ed. T. E. Lones (London, 1938),
ii. 136–57.

man, if the other were away.' Grace then gives the writing-tablets to the first man who comes along, asking him to choose between the two names. The first man who happens to come along is the madman Trouble-all. Madman is asked to act as judge; the moment mirrors for us the judge's acting as madman. But Trouble-all's choice requires no judgement at all, as he is presented with something like a handy-dandy choice between two closed fists.

The following scene brings forward yet another game; the game of Vapours which (Jonson explains in a side-note) *'is* non sense. *Euery man to oppose the last man that spoke: whether it concern'd him, or no.'* The game marks an ultimate in arbitrariness, in 'noise' and 'sport'; reason is quite suspended; language deteriorates into 'nonsense' (the *O.E.D.*'s first recorded use of the word)[1] rather in the way it does during the holiday games presided over by Moria in *Cynthia's Revels* and the 'jeering' games in the fourth act of *The Staple of News*.

> Wheresoever, manners, and fashions are corrupted, Language is. It imitates the publicke riote. The excesse of Feasts, and apparell, are the notes of a sick State; and the wantonnesse of language, of a sick mind.
>
> ... *Speech* is the only benefit man hath to expresse his excellencie of mind above other creatures. It is the instrument of *Society*.
>
> (*Discoveries*, 954–6; 1881–3)

The 'instrument of *Society*' is here untuned; 'the only benefit man hath to expresse his excellencie of mind above the other creatures' is reduced to mere 'vapours', as insignificant as the clouds of steam and smoke which fill the stage at frequent intervals. As the game reaches its pitch of confusion, '*They fall by the eares*', and Edgworth steals the licence out of Wasp's black box.

Throughout this fourth act of the play Jonson masterfully

[1] Cf. *Discoveries*, 1869.

thickens and complicates the plot. It is in the fifth act that the play's most spectacular reversals occur. In iv. i Justice Overdo is placed in the stocks. Here is a classic image of inverted authority. T. W. Craik has shown that the fettering of Justice (or of some other Virtue) in the stocks was a fairly common symbolic motif in Tudor interludes, and that it is also to be found in various artistic representations: Dürer in 1524, for instance, designed a tapestry showing Justice, Truth, and Reason in the stocks. Craik conjectures plausibly that the placing of Kent in the stocks in *King Lear* may possibly derive from this tradition: Jonson's scene (one might add) would appear to be even more obviously related to it.[1] Once again, the notion of legal freedoms and restraints is allowed to have wider reverberations, as Busy, also under arrest, proclaims: 'No, Minister of darknesse, no, thou canst not rule my tongue, my tongue it is mine own . . .' (iv. i. 91–2). His words recall Littlewit's conceits in the first scene of the play; they recall, too, with a pleasing contradiction, two different kinds of biblical texts: those which encourage the faithful to speak out boldly during times of persecution (e.g. Philippians 1:14), and those which roundly condemn ungoverned speech ('But the tongue can no man tame; it is an unruly evil, full of deadly poison', James 3:8). By the last scene of the fourth act all three 'governors', Overdo, Busy, and Wasp, find themselves in the stocks; this is the play's ultimate point of topsy-turvyness. And in the stocks Overdo, the make-believe madman, commends Trouble-all, the real madman, for his good sense.

While their men are thus variously occupied, all the women of the play are now at large. Just as Quarlous and

[1] T. W. Craik, *The Tudor Interlude* (Leicester, 1958), pp. 93–5. Since this chapter was written, Brian Gibbons has made the same connection in his *Jacobean City Comedy* (London, 1968).

Winwife have converged upon Grace, abandoned by Cokes, so now Whit and Knockem converge upon Win Littlewit and Mistress Overdo, both abandoned by their husbands, and both driven to Ursula's booth by (the crudest of comic levellers) the common need to urinate. And in Ursula's booth Mistress Overdo undergoes a punishment which parallels that of her husband in the stocks, as a whore (also called Alice) mistakes her for a rival in her trade: '*Alice enters, beating the Iustice's wife*' (IV. v. 60: note). Justice and thief, wife and whore, are all now humiliatingly levelled. At the end of the fourth act, with a final, brilliant twist, Jonson allows the last remaining female visitor to the Fair to break from her escort: Dame Purecraft, that 'most elect hypocrite', abandons Zeal-of-the-Land Busy for another, falling zealously in love with the madman Trouble-all.

The fifth act of *Bartholomew Fair* is Jonson's most subtle and extended dramatic treatment of the whole complex of ideas provoked by the comparison of real and theatrical life; with great ingenuity and humanity Jonson explores the truth that *hypocrisy* or play-acting is a universal, and not necessarily baleful, element in all human activity. The word 'hypocrite'—as one critic has pointed out[1]—had virtually become a cant name for a Puritan. And yet, as Puritan opponents of the stage were quick to remark, the word also had another sense:

A iust man cannot endure hypocrisie, but all the acts of Players is dissimulation, and the proper name of Player . . . is hypocrite. . . . *For* what else is *hypocrisie* in the proper signification of the word, *but the acting of anothers part or person on the Stage*: or what else is an *hypocrite, in his true etimologie, but a Stage-player, or one who acts anothers part . . .*[2]

[1] *Bartholomew Fair*, ed. Eugene M. Waith, ed. cit., Introduction, p. 10.
[2] William Prynne, *Histrio-Mastix, The Players Scovrge* (London, 1633), Part 1, Actus 4, Scena Prima, p. 141; Actus 5, Scena Prima, p. 158.

Puritans and players are hypocrites alike: this is to be the final, levelling stroke of the fifth act; yet it has been anticipated from the beginning of the play. Quarlous has described Busy as 'One that stands upon his face more than his faith', and his phrase may remind us that Jonson called that most consummate actor of *The Alchemist* by the name of Face. And in the first act Dame Purecraft's hypocrisy is matched by the counter-plotting of her daughter:

> *Littlewit.* I'll goe in and tell her, cut thy lace i' the meane time and play the *Hypocrite*, sweet *Win*.
> *Win.* No, I'll not make me vnready for it. I can be *Hypocrite* enough, though I were neuer so straight lac'd.   (I. v. 158–61)

Win's deception of her mother is matched in the fifth act, where Quarlous, learning that Winwife is to be the man for Grace, and that Purecraft has sunk her affection in Trouble-all, dons a robe and a beard and impersonates the madman himself; once again, with a neat poetic justice, hypocrisy is met by hypocrisy. As Quarlous puts on his disguise, Purecraft removes hers: 'I must vncover my selfe vnto him . . .' (v. ii. 48); and Overdo likewise reveals his disguise: 'I am the man, friend *Trouble-all*, though thus disguis'd (as the carefull *Magistrate* ought) for the good of the Republique in the *Fayre*, and the weeding out of enormity' (v. ii. 91–4). 'Can a ragged robe produce these effects?' Quarlous asks himself; and although the 'robe' is his own disguise, his words seem to take on a more general sense like Lear's 'robes and furred gowns hide all' that includes the judicial robe of Overdo as well. As all the characters of the play are now drawn towards the event which produces the final dramatic resolution, the puppet-show, the disguises have multiplied: Overdo is dressed now as a porter; the ladies are all masked; Littlewit has concealed his identity until he sees how his puppet-show is received; Busy is still wrapped in his self-deceptions. Only Cokes, now stripped of his hat and cloak, has the nakedness of foolish innocence. When Trouble-all finally enters with his cry *'be uncovered'*, the words seem to take on an extra dimension of meaning.

All acting involves, to a greater or lesser extent, a surrender of personal identity. Sometimes, as Jonson often shows, it can also involve a surrender of humanity: the Machiavellian 'actor' becomes like a lion or a fox, a mere beast. *Bartholomew Fair* presents a comic variation of this idea. The obsessive determination of men to act out their official roles—judge, puritan inquisitor, tutor, officer of the law—renders them as inhuman as the puppets of the Fair-ground. 'I know no fitter match', says Grace, 'then a *Puppet* to commit with an Hypocrite' (v. v. 50-1). Zeal-of-the-Land Busy's angry contention with the puppets derives, I think, from Cervantes's scene in which Don Quixote attacks Master Peter's pasteboard puppets[1] (see Plate 2); yet it also has a more savage irony of the kind found in Swift's *Mechanical Operation of the Spirit*. To Busy, the puppets as well as their masters are breakers of the law; and the words of his attack gather together the play's central notions of law, licence, and revelry, fixing them for us in two blatant puns:

> *Leatherhead.* Sir, I present nothing, but what is licens'd by authority.
> *Busy.* Thou art all *license*, even *licentiousnesse* it selfe, *Shemei!*
> *Leatherhead.* I haue the Master of the *Reuell*'s hand for it, Sir.
> *Busy.* The Master of the *Rebells* hand, thou hast; *Satan's!*
>
> (v. v. 14-20)

The puppet-show itself, and the following contention between Busy and the puppet Dionysius, give us the last 'games' of *Bartholomew Fair*; each deteriorates into the same sort of nonsense as the game of Vapours:

---

[1] *Don Quixote*, Part II, Ch. XXVI.

PLATE 2

Charles Antoine Coypel (1694–1752): Don Quixote demolishing the puppet-show.

Busy. Yet, I say, his *Calling*, his Profession is prophane, it is prophane, *Idoll.*

Puppet Dionysius. It is not prophane!

Leatherhead. It is not prophane, he sayes.

Busy. It is prophane.

Pup. Dionysius. It is not prophane.

Busy. It is prophane.

Pup. Dionysius. It is not prophane.

Leatherhead. Well said, confute him with *not*, still. You cannot beare him down with your base noyse, Sir.   (v. v. 67–76)

Between puppet and man there seems little to choose; it is no longer a matter of interchangeability of man and man, but of man and puppet. Yet the puppets, however much they may be made to mimic the actions of the characters themselves (the stage direction '*Heere the Puppets quarrell and fall together by the eares*', for instance, recalls the manner in which the game of Vapours has ended: '*They fall by the eares*') have one great advantage over men and women of flesh and blood. The puppets, as Leatherhead has pointed out, are 'a ciuill company' and 'well-gouern'd', as none of the human company is. And being themselves mere toys, they can be made to reproach others without fear that the reproach will return upon themselves. In 1633 the Puritan William Prynne, attacking stage plays and players, countered the argument that players might be said to serve a useful social purpose in reproaching other people for their vices, by pointing out that players 'have no authenticke commission, either from God or man' (no warrant or licence, one might say) to censure vice; this office was reserved for '*Magistrates, Ministers, and such like publike persons, who are deputed by God himselfe*'. And again, argued Prynne, this argument falls 'because Players are of all others, the unmeetest persons to reprove mens vices. *He, who will effectually rebuke the sinnes, the enormities of other men, must be free from open crimes himselfe*;

else his reproofes will want authority. . . .'[1] Jonson brilliantly enlarges this general proposition ('He that will correct another, must want fault in himselfe') so that it rebounds upon the Puritan himself; and the favourite Puritan argument that the players wear the apparell of the opposite sex[2] is confuted as the puppet reveals that these 'actors' have no sex, and (unlike their accusers) none of the sins of the flesh.

Throughout the play Adam Overdo's attacks on the vices of the Fair have closely parallelled those of Rabbi Busy; both men, for instance, have inveighed against the evils of ale and tobacco (II. vi, III. vi), and—as Jonas Barish has shown—the two men share certain verbal characteristics as they denounce such vanities. For Overdo, as for Busy, the puppets are 'licencious' (v. iii. 69), and it is fitting that Overdo is the next to descend in wrath, first silencing Littlewit with an exposure of the conduct of his wife ('*Redde te Harpocratem*', v. vi. 48) and then to be silenced himself as he observes the conduct of his own wife: '*Mistresse Ouerdoo is sicke: and her husband is silenc'd*' (v. vi. 67). Next Wasp is silenced ('I will neuer speak while I liue, againe, for ought I know': v. vi. 103–4), as Quarlous's remarks sweep across each governor in turn:

> Looke i' your boxe, *Numps*, nay, Sir, stand not you fixt here, like a stake in *Finsbury* to be shot at, or the whipping post i' the *Fayre*, but get your wife out o' the ayre, it will make her worse else; and remember you are but *Adam*, Flesh, and blood! you haue your frailty, forget your other name of *Ouerdoo*, and inuite vs all to supper.
>
> *Wasp misseth the License*
>
> (v. vi. 93–8)

'. . . remember you are but *Adam*, Flesh and blood': Christianity and farce are superbly blended in the play's

---

[1] Prynne, *Histrio-Mastix*, Part 1, Actus 3, Scena Sexta, p. 125.
[2] e.g. ibid., Part 1, Actus 5, Scena Sexta, pp. 178–216.

final levelling. And yet there is a curious sense that the play is still not over. 'Nay, I can be mad, sweet heart, when I please', says Quarlous to Purecraft (v. vi. 86), as he hands gown and cap back to Trouble-all; though the disguises are removed, play-acting will continue to serve those who have employed it in the past. 'Yes, and bring the *Actors* along,' says Cokes, 'wee'll ha' the rest o' the *Play* at home' (v. vi. 114–15). The puppet-play, of course; yet his words also give the sensation that the play itself has not decisively ended, but may continue later at Overdo's house in a kind of green-room party. Play-acting and real life have become inseparably intertwined.

II

One of Jonson's notable skills in this play is that of modulation of tone: the play is indignant and compassionate, farcical and serious in turn. The play's final moments, as I suggested in the first chapter, may once again put us in mind of *King Lear* ('Thou rascal beadle, hold thy bloody hand!'), yet the truth that no man is fit to judge another is enforced in a manner which, despite moments of graver irony elsewhere in the play, remains amused and comic. The ending of the play is more like that of *Cynthia's Revels* than that of *Volpone*: 'Since revells were proclaim'd let none now bleed.' And yet the play does not quite come to rest at a point of tolerant, festive anarchy. In the Court epilogue Jonson makes a gracious and serious return to the world of everyday law. 'The power to judge', the epilogue declares, is finally that of King James himself; and it is significant that the king is asked to judge not simply (as Charles is asked in the epilogue to *The Magnetic Lady*) whether the play is a good one or a bad one, but whether or not Jonson has abused his privilege as a writer, whether he has turned royal 'leaue' into 'licence'. The play's leading question is now turned against the writer of the play himself. The final appeal to the king re-affirms, with the lightest of touches, but nevertheless with something of the effect of the entry of the main masque after the anarchy of an anti-masque, the existence of a real and workable social order with James at its head.

And what would James have thought of this play? Commentators have in the past been quicker to detect allusions in Jonson's work that imply hostility to King James's policies (his excessive bestowal of knighthoods, for instance) than to detect those which imply admiration; yet in some cases further inquiry has shown that what look like uncomplimentary references to the king's activities are in fact the reverse.[1] It is sometimes felt that in one or two possible allusions to the king's policies and practices in *Bartholomew Fair* Jonson may have been sailing a bit close to the wind: Barish wondered how the author of *A Counterblast to Tobacco* would have taken a near-parody of his views in Overdo's extravagant condemnation of the evils of smoking in Act Two of the play; Gifford likewise had speculated on the propriety of depicting Rabbi Busy in disputation with a puppet, in view of the fact that James prided himself upon his formal disputations with leading Puritan divines.[2] The question of what was or was not dramatically decorous to set before the king is probably too delicate for us to attempt to decide at this distance in time; quite possibly Jonson felt he might have overstepped the mark here and there (hence the epilogue), but it would seem unlikely that in a play dedicated to the king and designed (partly, at least) for a royal occasion Jonson should have

[1] See, for example, G. L. Kittredge, 'King James and *The Devil is an Ass*', *Modern Philology*, ix (1911), pp. 195–209.

[2] Barish, op. cit., pp. 319–20, n. 23; *The Works of Ben Jonson*, ed. W. Gifford (London, 1816), iv. 540.

held James up to derision. It might be more reasonable to suspect that in the figure of Overdo (acting as he does at all times 'in Iustice name, and the Kings, and for the commonwealth!') Jonson is depicting with amusement, but also with sympathy to his king, one of the minor pestilences of the kingdom: the magistrate who officiously uses his authority to inveigh against a practice which James himself has declared was 'too low for the Law to looke on'.[1] Similarly, the full force of *Bartholomew Fair* is so obviously anti-Puritan that it would seem idle to look for covert sideswipes at James. The reference to James's clashes with the Puritans which Jonson makes in the prologue is clearly sympathetic:

> ... *whereof the petulant wayes*
> *Your selfe haue knowne, and haue bin vext with long.*

Aubrey reported that 'King James made him write against the Puritans, who began to be troublesome in his time'; yet it is worth remembering the comment of Jonson's editors, that upon such a topic the dramatist hardly needed a prompter: his king's attitude was his own.[2]

So far from gently satirizing royal notions in *Bartholomew Fair*, Jonson would appear to be giving them serious endorsement through the means of comedy. *Bartholomew Fair* is a comedy about extremism, or *overdoing*. The overdoing ranges from Busy's intemperance in food ('fast by the teeth, i' the cold Turkey'pye, i' the cupbord, with a great white loafe on his left hand, and a glasse of *Malmesey* on his right':

---

[1] *A Counterblast to Tobacco*, ed. E. Arber, English Reprints 2 (Edinburgh, 1884), p. 97. Possibly in Overdo's attack upon smoking Jonson also had an eye on D'Olive's praise of the practice in Chapman's *Monsieur D'Olive* (1607); cf. the details about tobacco smoke carving a third nostril so that the nose appears like the ace of clubs: *Bartholomew Fair*, II. vi. 46; *Monsieur D'Olive*, II. i (and cf. Rabelais, *Pantagruel*, Livre IV, Ch. ix; Sterne, *Tristram Shandy*, vol. iii, Ch. 32).

[2] Herford and Simpson, ed. cit. x. 171.

I. vi. 33–6) to Littlewit's verbal excesses ('ouerdoing' is what Quarlous calls it; and Winwife warns him not to 'ouer-buy' his wit: I. v. 74–9), and Wasp's quarrelsomeness (he is 'ouerparted': III. iv. 54). Even more centrally, the play is concerned with the overdoing of the governor, and the dangers of inquisitorial zeal. In designing this play partly for a royal occasion, it seems not improbable that Jonson may have remembered what James himself has written on this subject, turning, as he had turned once or twice already, to his king's famous treatise written for his son in the 1590s, which had been reprinted within a few days of Elizabeth's death in 1603, and again continually throughout King James's reign: *Basilikon Doron.*[1] In *Basilikon Doron* James continually stresses the need for the ruler to cultivate moderation, temperance, and self-knowledge:

he cannot be thought worthie to rule and command others, that cannot rule and dantone his own proper affections and unreasonable appetites . . .

. . . censure your selfe as sharply, as if ye were your owne enemie: *For if ye iudge your selfe, ye shall not be iudged,* as the Apostle saith . . .

The ruler must cultivate all the virtues, but chiefly

make one of the them, which is Temperance, Queen of all the rest within you. I mean not by the vulgar interpretation of Temperance, which consists in *gustu & tactu,* by the moderation of these two senses: but I mean of that wise moderation, that first commanding yourself, shall as Queen, command all the affections and passions of your mind.

D. J. Gordon has shown that Jonson echoes this passage in *The Haddington Masque,* 216–23;[2] he would seem to

[1] *Basilikon Doron,* ed. James Craigie, Early Scottish Texts Society (Edinburgh, 1944).

[2] D. J. Gordon, 'Ben Jonson's *Haddington Masque*: the Story and the Fable', *M.L.R.* xlii (1947), p. 181, n. 2.

echo it again in *Discoveries*, 1005–7: '. . . the Prince commands others, and doth himself. The wise *Licurgus* gave no law, but what he himselfe kept.' The same point is made repeatedly in a comic context in *Bartholomew Fair*. 'He that will correct another, must want fault in himselfe'; 'I am content to be in *abeyance*, Sir, and be gouern'd by you . . . but 'twill be expected, you should also gouerne your passions.'

James has a good deal to say in *Basilikon Doron* about the vexatiousness of Puritans 'that thinke it their honour to contend with Kings, & perturbe whole kingdoms' and who show 'contempt of the ciuill Magistrate, . . . breathing nothing but sedition and calumnies, aspyring without measure, rayling without reason, and making their owne imaginiations (without any warrant of the worde) the square of their conscience.' Zeal-of-the-Land Busy's contention with Leatherhead's puppet—like his defiance of Overdo's officers, and like Purecraft's confident claim to 'a warrant out of the word'—would seem nicely calculated to please James by playing comfortably along with his known prejudices. Yet there was more than mere calculation behind Jonson's endorsement of *Basilikon Doron*. He would have agreed profoundly with James's remarks about the ways in which the law must be administered with moderation; and the following passage from *Basilikon Doron* would seem of real importance to Jonson's theme in *Bartholomew Fair*. The laws, declared James, 'are ordained as rules of vertuous and sociall living, and not to be snares to trap your good subjects; and therefore the law must be interpreted . . . not to the literal sense thereof, *Nam ratio est anima legis*'. Jonson liked this sentiment enough to follow it in *Discoveries*, 1191–3: '. . . the mercifull *Prince* is safe in love, not in feare. He needs no Emissaries, Spies, Intelligencers, to intrap true Subjects.' Adam Overdo, calling continually upon the authority of Justice, King, and Commonwealth

as he lays his snares to intrap the King's subjects, out-
rageously offends against all his king had said about the
administration of Justice within the Commonwealth. Like
every other character in *Bartholomew Fair*, Overdo appeals
to a notion of law simply as a cover for his own excesses;
like every other character, he forgets his king's real advice:
'*Nam ratio est anima legis.*' His failure is, once again, one of
understanding.

Most of the sentiments which James expresses in *Basilikon
Doron* are thoroughly familiar and traditional ones; no one
would turn to the work for original ideas, and it is not so
much a case of Jonson's *borrowing* his king's ideas as of his
knowing what ideas he had, and shaping his comedy in a
general way around them. An occasional play demanded the
same tact as an occasional masque (obviously, for instance,
Jonson would have known when he wrote his holiday play
that James had defended in his treatise the observation of
holidays with their traditional 'feasting and merrinesse',
despite Puritan attacks on such customs). It seems quite
possible that in writing *Bartholomew Fair* partly for a royal
occasion, Jonson remembered an important precedent set
by his great rival in another play written for a royal occasion
ten years earlier. In *Measure for Measure*, it has been per-
suasively argued,[1] Shakespeare may have been prompted
to explore the problems of the uses of power and 'government' by his reading in this same treatise, newly reprinted
when James came to the throne the previous year. On
26 December 1604 King James was presented with a play
which, like *Bartholomew Fair*, subtly and humanely demon-
strated the virtue of self-knowledge in the governor. Duke
Vincentio is said to be

---

[1] See David L. Stevenson, 'The Role of James I in Shakespeare's *Measure
for Measure*', *ELH*, xxvi (1959), 188–208; Ernest Schanzer, *The Problem
Plays of Shakespeare* (London, 1962), Ch. 2; Josephine Waters Bennett,
'*Measure for Measure*' *as Royal Entertainment* (Columbia, 1966).

One, that above all other strifes,
Contended especially to know himself—
(III. ii. 226–7)

and one who affirms that the first duty of the ruler is, as James
had put it, to 'censure your selfe as sharply, as if ye were
your owne enemie':

More, nor less to other paying,
Than by self-offences weighing.
(III. ii. 258–9)

One almost senses a touch of parody in *Bartholomew Fair*:
Overdo, like Shakespeare's Duke, goes about in disguise
to spy upon corruption, leaving to his deputies the more
difficult task of actually enforcing the laws; like the Duke
he sees a society in which

. . . Liberty plucks Justice by the nose,
The baby beats the nurse, and quite athwart
Goes all decorum.   (I. iii. 29–31)

Like his near-namesake Mistress Overdone, Justice Overdo
is led not by moderation but a love of excess. Yet it would
be a mistake to see this simply as a case of minor dramatic
parody. Whether Jonson had *Measure for Measure* in mind
or not when writing *Bartholomew Fair* does not finally
matter very much; what does matter is an understanding
that Jonson succeeded in this play in dealing with serious
matters in the most farcical of modes. Like *Measure for
Measure* (though with quite different degrees of irony,
compassion, and humour) *Bartholomew Fair* takes as its
theme the recoil of the law upon those who attempt to ad-
minister it, and the surprising and perplexing consequences
of man's attempts to impose his authority over man. It is a
comic parable upon the same gospel text: *Judge not, that ye be
not judged.*

CHAPTER FOUR

'Living Backward': *The Antipodes*

'...and pray what is Man, but a topsy-turvy Creature, his
Animal Faculties perpetually mounted on his Rational, his
Head where his Heels should be, groveling on the Earth!'
JONATHAN SWIFT, *A Meditation upon a Broomstick.*

I

IN Jonson's comedies it is often the clever man, not the
good man, who comes out on top. It is tempting to speak
of the wryness, the open-endedness, the modernity of
Jonson's work. And yet one does not have to read very
far in the plays to be aware of Jonson's fondness for sharp
and severe moral contrasts. As in the Psychomachia drama of
an earlier age, vice may be pitted against virtue, the evil life
may parody and reverse the good life. A Moria, a Sejanus,
a Morose embody moral qualities directly opposed to those
which the good man should emulate. Folly and wickedness
are expressed in terms of moral contrariness. The idea is
outlined with particular clarity in the *Discoveries* (549–58):

How many have I knowne, that would not have their vices
hid? Nay, and to be noted, live like *Antipodes* to others in the
same *Citie*; never see the Sunne rise, or set, in so many yeares;
but be as they were watching a Corps by Torch-light; would
not sinne the common way, but held that a kind of *Rusticity*; they
would doe it new, or contrary, for the infamy? They were
ambitious of living backward; and at last arrived at that, as they
would love nothing but the vices; not the vicious customes.

The geographical image—'live like *Antipodes*' (that is, like
antipodeans)—precisely suggests the strong moral polarity

of Jonson's thought.[1] Between a Volpone and a Celia, between a Catiline and a Cicero, between the witches of *The Masque of Queenes*—those 'opposites to good *Fame*', who 'do all thinges contrary to the custome of Men'—and the ladies of that masque who represent true heroical virtue, there can be no real meeting; such figures inhabit opposite sides of the moral globe, antipodeans to each other. The sharp contrasts afforded by Court masque and antimasque evidently suited such a moral temperament as Jonson's. In a muted form, the contrasts are to be found, too, in Jonson's early comedies, though they are less obvious in the more sophisticated comedies of his maturity; there is no Crites, no Cordatus, no Celia in either *Epicoene* or *Bartholomew Fair* to offer us the luxury of a moral alternative or point of rest. Yet even in these plays, Jonson's conceptualizations of the nature of folly and evil have not changed: folly and evil still invert the good life; the embittered solitariness of Morose stands in exact contrast to those qualities of open hospitality which Jonson praises, for example, in the Sidney family ('To Penshurst'); the officiousness of Overdo travesties King James's ideal of the true offices of the ruler; and it is significant that the two plays should remind us at points of the more formalized depictions of moral contrariness that Jonson presents in *Hymenaei* and *Time Vindicated to Himself and to his Honours*.

Richard Brome, mentioned apprehensively by the Stage-Keeper in *Bartholomew Fair* as Jonson's 'man',[2] absorbed the principles of his master's art with a devotion not even

---

[1] See Edward Partridge's perceptive discussion of this aspect of Jonson's work in *The Broken Compass*, Chapter Four. For a closely similar use of the figure of the antipodes used in this passage in the *Discoveries*, cf. Chapman's *Monsieur D'Olive*, I. i, and *The Widow's Tears*, v. ii; and Samuel Butler, 'A Duke of Bucks', in *Characters and Passages from Note-Books*, ed. A. R. Waller (Cambridge, 1908), pp. 32–3.

[2] R. J. Kaufmann discusses the significance of this term in his *Richard Brome, Caroline Dramatist* (New York and London, 1961), pp. 19 ff.

Shadwell was to equal. Jonsonian characters, jokes, jibes, and turns of plot are strewn, not always with discrimination, throughout Brome's comedies. Like Jonson, Brome is fond of shaping his comedies around a central idea of moral contrariness. *The Late Lancashire Witches*, for instance, a comedy written in collaboration with Thomas Heywood in 1634, takes for its central, polarizing device a current scandal, the alleged witchcraft activities of certain Lancashire women, recently brought to London for trial.[1] Brome's and Heywood's witches, like those in *The Masque of Queenes*, turn normal life the wrong way about. They have turned one family, named Seely, quite upside-down; the family roles are now reversed: son commands father, daughter commands mother, servants command children. 'Indeed,' comments a neighbour, 'they say old men become children againe, but before I would become my childes childe, and make my foot my head, I would stand upon my head, and kick my heels at the skies' (I. i). A wedding is bewitched, and lapses (like that of Epicoene and Morose) into strife and discord, as the musicians play '*Every one a severall tune*', and a skimmington visits the bridal pair. Various forms of discord and absurdity continue throughout five acts until the witches are finally brought to justice, and order is restored to Lancashire. In *The Antipodes* (acted 1638) Brome turned to another cluster of popular beliefs and superstitions which allowed for equally sharp comic contrasts between virtue and iniquity, normality and absurdity. This time the play's unifying device is not religious but geographical.

The Antipodes shows off well enough the kind of dramatic skill which Brome had; a skill in what might be called light-weight structural engineering, fairly obviously derived from the richer skills of his master in comedy, Jonson. With

---

[1] G. E. Bentley, *The Jacobean and Caroline Stage* (Oxford, 1941–56), iii. 74.

James Shirley, Brome is today the most readable of the
Caroline comic dramatists; his plays are brisk, well-made,
seldom dull. Seldom, on the other hand, are Brome's
plays ever distinguished by true comic originality: his
talent is never more than an engaging minor one. The
notion upon which *The Antipodes* is based—that upon the
southern side of the globe manners and morals are exactly
contrary to those upon the northern side—has generally
been taken to be Brome's own.[1] The interest of the comedy
in fact consists not in the originality of the notion but in
its familiarity. So usual was the association of the antipodes
with absurdity that by Brome's day the phrase *to act the
antipodes* had become a proverbial expression for a reversal
of the expected order of things. Only a few years after the
performance of Brome's play, an anonymous writer lamented
the upheavals of Civil War in these words: 'But now the
world is turned upside downe, and all are acting the
Antipodes, young boyes command old Souldiers, wise men
stand cap in hand to fine fooles, maidens woe widowes,
married women rule their husbands . . . It was not so in
Temporibus Noah, ah no.'[2] It is not difficult to see how the

---

[1] Felix Schelling's opinion that in this play 'Brome conceived an original
notion' (*The Elizabethan Drama* (Boston and New York, 1908) has been
echoed by later commentators. C. E. Andrews, after a lengthy search through
earlier literature dealing with the antipodes, declares that he has 'not been
able to find that any such idea [of topsyturvydom] was ever associated with
the antipodes before the date of this play' (*Richard Brome: A Study of his Life
and Works*, Yale Studies in English, vol. xlvi (New York, 1913), p. 115).
R. J. Kaufmann says: 'The device around which the play is organized is, I
believe, quite original' (op. cit., p. 64), and A. S. Knowland agrees that 'it
is possible that one stumbles upon that refreshing thing in the drama of the
time, an original conception' (*Six Caroline Plays* (London, 1962), p. ix).

[2] *Pigges Corantoe*, p. 7, cited in C. R. Baskervill, *The Elizabethan Jig* (Chicago,
1929), p. 58 n. 1. Compare the famous concluding paragraph to *The Garden
of Cyrus*, which so irritated Coleridge, in which Browne declared that the
orderliness of his treatise is threatened by the coming of night, 'the daughter
of Chaos': 'To keep our eyes open longer were but to act our Antipodes'
(*The Works of Sir Thomas Browne*, ed. Geoffrey Keynes (London, 1928), i. 226).

association arose. The very idea that the antipodes might exist seemed at first quite absurd enough in itself. If the antipodes exist, ran the traditional objections, where then is hell? And what of the staggering physical problems involved?

> For if men, on opposite sides, placed the soles of their feet each against each, whether they chose to stand on earth or water, or air or any kind of body, how could both be found standing upright? The one would assuredly be found in the natural upright position and the other, contrary to nature, head downwards. Such notions are opposed to reason and alien to our nature and constitution.[1]

From such grave philosophical ponderings as these arose the popular facetious image of the antipodeans walking upside-down: Brome's Quailpipe is to speak the prologue to the play-within-the-play with his beaver hat 'Upon his feet, and on his head shooe-leather'; and years later Henry Carey, searching for an ultimate absurdity in his burlesque play *Chrononhotonthologos* (1733), introduces a King of the Antipodes, who walks—predictably—upon his hands.[2] When the Renaissance voyages of discovery had finally confirmed the hypotheses of the astronomers, and the existence of the antipodes was at last proved to be true, it was still the topsyturvyness of affairs in those parts which, naturally enough, caught the attention of the early commentators. 'Yet haue we nothinge common wyth them, but all thinges contrarye', wrote Richard Eden of the antipodeans in his prefatory epistle to his translation of

---

[1] Cosmas Indicopleustes, *Christian Topography*, ed. J. W. McCrindle, Hakluyt Society, Old Series, vol. 98 (London, 1897), p. 17.

[2] The King is depicted in his uncomfortable position in a design for the frontispiece to the first edition of the play, attributed to Henri Gravelot (reproduced in V. C. Clinton-Baddeley's *The Burlesque Tradition in the English Theatre After 1660* (London, 1952), facing p. 68). Another King of the Antipodes is to be found in the anonymous play of *Timon, c.* 1600.

Münster's *Cosmographie*; 'for when the Sunne causeth Sommer wyth vs, then it is Myddewynter wyth them: and when it is day wyth vs, then is the longeste nyghte wyth them, and the shorteste daye.'[1] Seasonal contrariness might be seen as an index of a profounder contrariness of customs and morals.

One small zoological discovery in the antipodes aroused particular interest throughout Europe. Ever since Juvenal had declared in his sixth satire that a chaste wife was a *rara avis in terris nigroque simillima cycno*, the black swan had been taken as a familiar symbol of anything absurdly contrary to common observation. 'What man is so mad as wil say the swan is black?' asked one writer in 1576; and Gosson in his *School of Abuse* three years later pronounced that the theatres were places of such corruption 'that for any chaste liuer to haunt them was a black swan, and a white crow'.[2] And in 1638 Brome's play was to raise an easy laugh at Salisbury Court as one of its characters, inquiring about life at the antipodes, asked the expected question: 'Are not their Swannes all blacke, and Ravens white?' Two years earlier, unknown to the play's author and its audience, Antonie Caen, skipper of the *Banda*, reported that he had seen near Bernier Island two birds which seemed to be none other than the legendary black swans: the first time that these common birds of the antipodes had been sighted by Europeans. It was not until the end of the century, when members of the Royal Society were informed that a Dutch captain had caught four of

---

[1] Richard Eden, '*A treatyse of the newe* India . . .', in *The First Three English Books on America*, ed. Edward Arber (Birmingham, 1885), p. 10.

[2] *Cit. O.E.D.* under entry 'swan'. Cf. Jonson's 'Ode ἀλληγορικὴ' (Herford and Simpson, ed. cit. viii. 366: 'Who saith our Times not haue, nor can / Produce vs a blacke Swan?' Cf. also Browne, *Pseudodoxia Epidemica*, v. 19, in *Works*, ed. cit. ii. 379; and Locke, *An Essay Concerning Human Understanding*, Bk. II, Ch. xxiii, §14, ed. A. C. Fraser (Oxford, 1894), i. 405.

these extraordinary birds in Western Australia and taken them alive to Batavia, that the existence of the antipodean black swan became known in England.[1] The discovery must have provided satisfactory confirmation of popular ideas about the contrariness of things on the other side of the earth.

Such notions about the contrariness of the New World— based sometimes upon traditional speculation, sometimes upon actual reports of the sea-voyagers—provided tempting material for comic, fantastic, and utopian treatment: *Gulliver's Travels* brilliantly crowns a long literary tradition.[2] Voyages to America, and even more wonderfully to the sun and moon, provided a location from which to look back upon European manners with a quizzical and comparative eye. The imaginary voyage to the antipodes, that traditional seat of absurdity, allowed for the sharpest and most spectacular of contrasts. As early as Mandeville, geographical opposites had naturally suggested moral opposites: with the grave air of the comparative anthropologist, Mandeville chronicled the habits of the people of the land of Lamary, who live 'feet agen feet' with those in the civilized north; these people think it proper to wear no clothes, sleep with each other's wives, hold all their goods and land in common, and practise cannibalism; all things contrary and abhorrent to the thinking of northerners.[3] Later writers developed more improbable antipodean

---

[1] *Philosophical Transactions of the Royal Society* (London, 1698), xx. 361; D. L. Serventy and H. M. Whittell, *Birds of Western Australia* (Perth, 1962), p. 16.

[2] W. A. Eddy, *'Gulliver's Travels': A Critical Study* (Princeton, 1923); R. W. Frantz, 'Swift's Yahoos and the Voyagers', *M.P.* xxix (1931), pp. 49 ff.; Marjorie Hope Nicolson, *Voyages to the Moon* (New York, 1948); Geoffroy Atkinson, *Nouveaux horizons de la renaissance française* (1935); P. B. Gove, *The Imaginary Voyage in Prose Fiction* (New York, 1941).

[3] *Mandeville's Travels*, ed. P. Hamelius, E.E.T.S. Original Series, No. 153 (London, 1919) Ch. xxi pp. 118 ff.

fantasies. William Bullein in his *Dialogue Against the Fever Pestilence* (1594) anticipated several features of Brome's play: Bullein's Mendax, an eccentric buffoon, entertains a company in an inn during a time of plague with an account of his travels to the antipodes:

> Then came I iust upon our Antipodie, foote against foote, in a land like ours, and al had been in one climate, of Riuers, Hilles, and Valies like ours. There is Gaddes hill, Stangate hole, Newe Market heath, like ours in all pointes; Also countries like Wales, Tinsdale, and Riddesdale; sauing there were some true men but here is scant one in them, I trowe, in Tinsdale.[1]

Just as Peregrine in Brome's play is to come upon the city of anti-London in the antipodes, so Mendax discovers Nodnol (London, back-to-front) in Taerg Natrib (Great Britain); in this 'best reformed Citie of this woorld' there are wise judges and no criminals, the sabbath is strictly observed, hospitality flourishes, the people are noted for their virtue and the courtiers for their 'verie curtesie'. Joseph Hall's *Mundus Alter et Idem* (1605) reveals an anti-podean land called Moronia where life is organized in an altogether less orthodox way: here fools are revered as wise men, and the women rule the men; the people wear heavy clothes at the height of summer, and in winter go almost naked.[2]

Such simple antipodean fantasies as these evidently cost their authors little in the way of imaginative exertion. They have a sense of having slipped easily and predictably from the pen, playing with notions of unconventionality in thoroughly conventional ways, laying bare certain areas of

[1] William Bullein, *A Dialogue Against the Fever Pestilence*, ed. Mark W. Bullen (London, 1888), E.E.T.S. Extra series, No. 52, p. 105.

[2] Joseph Hall, *Mundus Alter et Idem*, in his *Works*, ed. Philip Wynter (London, 1863), x. 399–495; later translated into English as *The Discovery of a New World or a Description of the South Indies. Hetherto Vnknowne*, 'By an English Mercury' (London, n.d.).

traditional lore and humour. Like these works, Brome's play moves lightly and undemandingly, though with some intricacy of design, over familiar comic territory. And it is, arguably, in this respect that the play is most worth attention: to read *The Antipodes* is to feel in touch with a kind of mid-seventeenth-century folk humour. To read *The Antipodes* after reading *Epicoene* or *Bartholomew Fair* is to feel the very great distance between an original, unsettling writer of dramatic genius for whom the sharp contrasts provided by such folk humour were simply an occasional means of anchoring more turbulent and complex feelings, and his neat and competent imitator, for whom they could become an end in themselves.

II

The action of *The Antipodes* takes place in the city of London (where the Salisbury Court theatre itself was situated) in the year of its performance, 1638. London had recently been visited by the plague; the theatres had been closed between May 1636, and October 1637 in an attempt to check its spread.[1] Like Jonson in *The Alchemist*, Brome shapes the play's ideas around the central notion of the plague. In the play's opening scene the herald-painter Blaze welcomes to his London house an old country gentleman, Joyless:

> To me, and to the City, Sir, you are welcome,
> And so are all about you: we have long
> Suffer'd in want of such faire Company.

The speech functions as a quasi-prologue, for those 'all about' Joyless include the Londoners who have come to this theatre to watch this very play; Blaze's 'we' likewise includes the actors themselves, who have suffered 'long on

[1] Bentley, op. cit. ii. 661–5.

the plankes of sorrow' because of the theatre closure;
after the sorrowful visit of the plague, the visit of this
audience—like the visit of the Joyless family to London—
will bring a new 'joy':

> Be comforted good Sir, my house, which now
> You may be pleas'd to call your owne, is large
> Enough to hold you all; and for your sorrowes,
> You came to lose 'hem: And I hope the meanes
> Is readily at hand . . .

The 'house' is Blaze's house, and it is also Salisbury Court;
comedy is to be 'the meanes' by which the Joyless family,
like the Londoners themselves, will lose their sorrows.
Melancholy and madness need to be expelled, just as the
plague has been; the 'doctor', whose visit Blaze promises,
symbolically represents the dramatist himself, dealing in the

> . . . medicine of the minde, which he infuses
> So skilfully, yet by familiar wayes,
> That it begets both wonder and delight
> In his observers, while the stupid patient
> Finds health at unawares.

Joyless's son, Peregrine, has gone out of his mind in
Quixotic style, through excessive reading; not, in this case,
of books of romance, but of books of travel: Peregrine is
obsessed with travellers' tales of the manners and customs
practised at the antipodes. But the play's madness is not
confined to Peregrine; those most concerned for his health
are themselves in need of cure; as in *Bartholomew Fair*,
those in control are no better and no saner than those in
their charge. From the central, spectacular madness of
Peregrine other subtler forms of madness radiate out; his
antipodean obsession serves as a central comic symbol,
highlighting the play's other reversals in social and domestic relationships. Peregrine's wife, Martha, has gone out of

her mind after three years of still-unconsummated marriage;
Joyless, racked with suspicions of his own young wife,
Diana, is a victim to 'horn-madness'; Diana's own madness,
contrary to the chaste suggestions of her name, seems nothing short of nymphomania: while Peregrine suffers from
'travelling thoughts', Diana's complaint is her 'wandering
looke' (i. ii; i. vi). All are—in the traditional phrase—
acting the antipodes to their own true natures. Although they
do not yet know it, each member of the family is to be
subjected in turn to Doctor Hughball's curing arts, which
Blaze now describes to Joyless:

> . . . tother day
> He set the braines of an Attorney right,
> That were quite topsie turvy overturn'd
> In a pitch ore the Barre; so that (poore man)
> For many Moones, he knew not whether he
> Went on his heels or's head, till he was brought
> To this rare Doctor, now he walkes againe,
> As upright in his calling, as the boldest
> Amongst 'hem.

The metaphorical phrases take life from the play's central
image of the antipodes: the ironical 'upright' is a triple
pun, for physical, mental, and moral stability. The antipodean conceit pervades the play.

Nor is the madness and melancholy of *The Antipodes*
confined to Joyless and his family; as the play unfolds,
other varieties of mania and eccentricity are revealed.
Doctor Hughball lives with one Letoy, 'an odde Lorde in
towne, that lookes like no Lord', who dresses like a pedlar
and lives like an emperor, takes a pedantic interest in
heraldry and genealogies, and—to satisfy an extravagant
'humour'—keeps in his house a company of 'mad Grigs',
private retainers who entertain him with their acrobatics,
fencing, acting, music, and dancing. As the play's circles

of madness and eccentricity widen, so too do its circles of
illusion. Letoy's house, 'an Amphitheater / Of exercise and
pleasure' (i. v), forms the setting for another comedy of
Letoy's devising, designed to restore the spectators to their
senses: the comedy is to be called 'the world turn'd upside-
downe'. The play—ostensibly for the benefit of Peregrine
alone, but in fact acting upon a wider circle of spectators—
is to depict life as it is lived at the antipodes; Peregrine,
drugged by Doctor Hughball and then newly awakened,
will believe that he has really travelled to the other side of
the earth. The manners of the country at which he arrives
(Hughball warns him) will be 'Extreamely contrary' to
those he knows in his own country. In the antipodes the
people govern the magistrate, children and servants command their parents and masters, the women rule the men:
the wives go hawking and hunting, leaving the 'tittle-
tattle duties' to their husbands. Old men marry young
girls, young boys marry old women; the conventions of
courtship and even of sexual intercourse are reversed:[1]

> *Doctor.* But there the maids doe woe
> The Batchelors, and tis most probable,
> The wives lie uppermost.
>   *Diana.*   That is a trim,
> Upside-downe Antipodian tricke indeed. (i. vi)

Parrots teach their mistresses to talk; wild animals are
hunted by tame animals; lawyers are honest; and the
actors are all Puritans.

The play-within-the-play, acted by Letoy's men, presents
in a series of short scenes a number of absurdities of this
kind. The absurdities may remind us not only of those

---

[1] Cf. Edward Howard's Amazonian comedy *The Six Days' Adventure, or
the New Utopia* (1671). The association of sexual irregularity with the antipodes was commonplace; see, for instance, 'Cupid Far Gone' in *The Poems
of Richard Lovelace*, ed. C. H. Wilkinson (Oxford, 1925), p. 153 (I am obliged
to Mr. Tony Gibbs for drawing my attention to this poem).

popularly depicted in illustrations of 'the world upside down', but also of many of the classic absurdities of stage comedy. Justice goes backwards in the antipodes: the officers of the law flee before the criminal, who begs to be arrested; an anarchical judge subverts the very bases of justice. Age and youth change places in the antipodes: old men are dispatched to school, and are disciplined by the young. Men and women exchange roles in the antipodes: a wife commands her husband, a lady rake accosts innocent men upon the streets, while a militaristic 'Buff Woman' swaggers about in search of quarrels; a 'man-scold' must be ducked for his unseemly talkativeness. This swift series of archetypal comic scenes, as simple and immediate in their suggestions as chapbook icons, call up other more elaborate scenes. Captain Otter beaten by his wife, Adam Overdo stocked by his own officers, inhabit the same inverted world.

The simplicity of the inner play is offset by the complexity of the outer play. The inner play has five rings of spectators. Peregrine is the play's closest and most enthralled spectator; not having seen a play before, he fails to perceive (as Cokes likewise failed to perceive in *Bartholomew Fair*) where real life ends and feigned life begins. Unaware that it is a play that he is watching, Peregrine enters freely into the action, finally breaking into the players' properties-room, where he takes stock of all

Our statues and our images of Gods; our Planets and our
    constellations
Our Giants, Monsters, Furies, Beasts, and Bug-Beares,
Our Helmets, Shields, and Vizors, Haires, and Beards,
Our Pastbord March-paines, and our Wooden Pies.   (III. v)

Thinking himself to be in an enchanted castle, Peregrine rushes among the monsters, strikes them to the ground, takes prisoner the puppets, hacks the devils' masks to pieces, and finally, discovering a king's crown and robes, declares himself King of the Antipodes. Like Busy's contention with the puppets in Act Five of *Bartholomew Fair*, this scene also recalls Don Quixote's attack on Master Peter's puppets (see Plate 2). Peregrine is the forerunner of a favourite character type of the Restoration stage, the naïve country visitor to the playhouse who interprets literally the action he sees: a type Fielding was to bring to perfection in Partridge, shaken by fear of the ghost in Garrick's *Hamlet*.[1] In the second ring of spectators of 'The World Turn'd Upside-Downe' are Martha, Joyless, and Diana; only marginally more sophisticated and objective viewers, they too become increasingly involved in the play's action. Martha volunteers to go to bed with one of the actors who catches her fancy ('Shee's in the *Antipodes* too'), but is finally persuaded to find a better bedfellow, the King of the Antipodes himself: innocent of the deceptions involved, husband and wife at last come together as they should.[2] Diana, too, is taken by the good looks of the actors, and also by the accounts of the liberal sexual customs practised at the antipodes; her exclamations of delight draw constant attention to the tyranny she enjoys over her own husband, relating the situation of the inner play to that of the play without.

> The aire of *London*
> Hath tainted her obedience already

[1] *Tom Jones*, Bk. XVI, Ch. v. In Elkanah Settle's *The New World in the Moon* (1697), Tom Dawkins, newly arrived in town with his mother, visits the playhouse; watching a play in rehearsal, he believes that the figure of Cynthia is a princess, in love with him. Dawkins is a variant on the type Buckingham created in *The Rehearsal* with Smith, the sceptical visitor from the country, who refuses to accept the absurd theatrical conventions he is presented with, and comments upon them with blunt common sense.

[2] In Settle's *The Playhouse Wedding* (1711) and Gay's *The What D'Ye Call It* (1715) a similar deception is practised not upon the principals of the play-within-the-play but upon its spectators, as a stage marriage turns out to be a real one.

exclaims Joyless (II. iii); and we remember that the air of London, unlike the country air from which Joyless and Diana have come, has been tainted by the plague. The journey from the country to London, like Peregrine's 'journey' from London to anti-London, leads apparently to deeper sickness, but will finally prove to be a journey into health. The two journeys are linked in our minds by Hughball's words about the 'aire' of anti-London:

> But now we are come into a temperate clime
> Of equall composition of elements
> With that of *London*; and as well agreeable
> Unto our nature, as you have found that aire.   (II. iv)

In the third ring of spectators are Blaze and his wife Barbara. They are knowing spectators, aware of the purpose of the play, appointed to keep an eye on Martha, and even to enter in a minor way into the action itself: Blaze plays two 'mute' parts in the play-within-the-play. But Blaze and Barbara are themselves barely cured of the same diseases from which Joyless and Diana now suffer, jealousy and infidelity; their situation, too, finds its comic distorting mirror in the inner play, and like the country visitors they are

> . . . not alone
> Spectators, but (as we will carry it) Actors
> To fill your Comicke Scenes with double mirth.   (II. i)

In the fourth ring of spectators are Letoy and the doctor themselves, who enter the action from time to time to exchange quick confidences with their actors; for them, as for the fifth ring of spectators, the audience in the actual theatre of Salisbury Court, there is the pleasure of overseeing the inner play and its effect upon the more involved spectators. As in Molière's *L'Impromptu de Versailles*, the total effect is like that of Chinese boxes.

And yet it is of Pirandello (the Pirandello of *Enrico IV*) that one is most strongly reminded as the notion of *playing* takes on wider dimensions of meaning. The playing of Letoy's men, like that of the other actors of London,[1] has suffered as a result of the long theatre closure; the actors themselves (it is said) have been 'in the *Antipodes*', 'sunke past rising' (II. ii). In his Hamlet-like address to the players before the play-within-the-play begins, Letoy coaches his actors back to their true form, reminding them of the extravagances of acting style which they must strictly avoid:

> Ile none of these absurdities in my house,
> But words and action married so together,
> That shall strike harmony in the eares and eyes
> Of the severest, if judicious, Criticks.   (II. ii)

To banish *absurdities*, and to bring in *harmony* is—as the final masque will remind us—the movement and purpose of the whole play: the 'cure' is to spread to the actors themselves. But while the inner play (or 'By-play', as it is called) is proceeding, another kind of 'byplay' is taking place amongst the spectators: Letoy is openly courting Diana:

> Yes, Lady, this was Prologue to the Play,
> As this to sweet ensuing pleasures.   *Kisse*   (II. v)

Psychotherapy, as Pirandello makes plain in *Enrico IV*, may involve the same kind of play-acting and sustained pretences as does madness itself; we may be as teased by the problem of 'sincerity' as much in a doctor (and his colleague) as in a madman. Whether Letoy's courtship of Diana is a self-interested act or part of his larger strategy of cure, whether or not it is what he calls 'faire play' (III. i) remains in doubt right until the play's last act, to be resolved only by the play's closing rash of strawberry-mark revelations.

[1] So the actors themselves evidently thought: see Bentley, op. cit. ii. 664.

The simple theory upon which Letoy's and Hughball's cure is based is the same theory upon which Brome's comedy is based: *one fire drives out one fire; one nail, one nail*; absurdity expels absurdity. The antipodean 'byplay', presenting to Peregrine the things he imagined he most wished to see, forces him to see them not as desirable but as repugnant, driving him steadily back to normality, as his shocked interjections begin to show:

> —Call you this justice? (IV. iii)
>
> —Can men and women be so contrary
>   In all that we hold proper to each sex? (IV. iv)
>
> —Tis monstrous, this. (IV. ix)

and finally,

> —*Will you make me mad?* (IV. viii)

Diana's cure follows the same pattern. The inner play over, the guests retire for the night in Letoy's house, and Diana (like Peregrine) is suddenly faced with that which she thought she most wanted: in this case, an ardent suitor. Presented at last with Letoy's actual proposition, Diana actually recoils, to take up a shocked and thoroughly orthodox moral position:

> The very name
> Of husband, rightly weigh'd, and well remembred,
> Without more Law or discipline, is enough
> To governe womankinde in due obedience. . . . (V. iv)

And as Joyless, spying upon his wife, witnesses her loyalty, the cure of the whole family is brought to completion. The play's concluding masque, presented by Letoy's actors, formally represents the movement of the entire play: Discord and her followers (Folly, Jealousy, Melancholy, and Madness) are banished by Harmony and her followers (Mercury, Cupid, Bacchus, and Apollo); Discord's '*Song in untunable notes*'—reminiscent of the discordant wedding music in *Epicoene* and *The Late Lancashire Witches*—is replaced by the song of Harmony, concluding with the invitation to the play's final, symbolic dance of order:

> *Then let us revell it while we are here,*
> *And keep possession of this Hemisphere.*

'And keep possession of this Hemisphere': the phrase returns us to the play's central geographical metaphor. Reason in the little world of man must dominate over unreason, as in the greater world the upper hemisphere physically dominates the lower hemisphere. Lear's words come to mind:

> But to the girdle do the Gods inherit
> Beneath is all the fiend's: there's hell, there's darkness,
> There is the sulpherous pit. . . .[1]

Or as Sir Thomas Browne was to tease out the metaphor more explicitly in his *Christian Morals*:

Be not under any Brutal metempsychosis while thou livest, and walkest about erectly under the scheme of Man. In thine own circumference, as in that of the Earth, let the Rational Horizon be larger than the sensible, and the Circle of Reason than of Sense. Let the Divine part be upward; and the Region of Beast below. Otherwise 'tis but to live invertedly, and with thy Head unto the Heels of thy Antipodes.[2]

It seems reasonable, as I have suggested, to assume that Brome's own ideas about the function and purpose of comedy correspond closely to the ideas he gives to

[1] The 'girdle' of this passage is both the belt of a woman's garment, and, presumably, the equatorial line (cf. related usages in *A Midsummer Night's Dream*, II. i. 175–6; *Bussy D'Ambois*, I. i. 23; and see G. Whitney, *A Choice of Emblems* (Leyden, 1586), p. 203 (C2)). The allusion is to the older cosmology which denied the existence of the antipodes, and considered that hell and darkness were on the other side of the earth.

[2] Browne, ed. cit. i. 144.

Hughball and Letoy. His comedy, like theirs, takes us briefly into a world of exotic and abnormal ways in order to return us more decisively to the world of homely, familiar, and normal ways: one critic has aptly described this as a 'theory of comic catharsis'.[1] The interest of this theory, however, like the interest of the conceit upon which the play is built, lies not so much in its originality as in its commonness. The medical metaphor is a commonplace of comedy; the comparison of the comic dramatist to a physician, lancing sores, and probing wounds, is particularly familiar in 'humours' comedy, with its notions of individual 'disease' and purging. Jonson had given the theory of catharsis a grotesquely literal rendering in the final act of *Poetaster*, where Crispinus is given his violent emetic. To stress the importance of everyday conventions by turning them temporarily inside-out is likewise, as we have noticed, a function which comedy frequently shares with ritual. In the Induction to *The Taming of the Shrew*, for instance, Christopher Sly is solemnly told that his doctors have concluded that his blood has congealed because of his excessive sadness, and that he must be cured by watching 'a pleasant Comedy'. And in the play he watches, Kate's shrewishness is cured just as Peregrine's madness is cured in *The Antipodes*, by forcing it further in the direction of absurdity to which it has been tending: 'He kills her in her own humour', says Peter. *The Taming of the Shrew* is built, like *The Antipodes*, upon a series of reversals: a rogue dresses as a lord, a page dresses as his wife, a girl acts as if she were a man—and is finally cured through 'contraries', being forced to confess that the moon

---

[1] J. L. Davis, 'Richard Brome's Neglected Contribution to Comic Theory', *Studies in Philology*, xi (1943), pp. 520–8. Inga-Stina Ewbank has suggested that this play may be an offshoot of 'therapeutic' masques such as Fletcher's *The Mad Lover*, and *The Lover's Melancholy*: see *A Book of Masques* (Cambridge, 1967), p. 437 n. 1.

shines in the middle of the afternoon, and that an old man is a comely young girl—a master changes places with his servant, and a father is turned away by his son's servants. Like *The Antipodes*, though less simply, the comedy tends paradoxically to affirm the importance of the everyday relationships it appears to be flouting.

Unlike many absurdist plays of the modern theatre, *The Antipodes* is not designed to suggest to its audience the absurdity of everyday life; its tendency, on the contrary, is basically comforting and conservative. The moral premisses of the play are strikingly simple and assured; the play does not explore or challenge orthodox ideas about social relationships, but takes it for granted that these ideas are not in dispute. The absurdities Brome gives to his antipodes are simply mirror-reversals of the accepted ways in which social relationships ought to work. Unlike a Montaigne, a Locke, a Swift, Brome does not allow his notions of the customs of the new world to unsettle our confidence in the customs of the old world: the inhabitants of anti-London are never anything other than absurd; the very exaggeration of the reversals in that city reassure an audience that familiar ways are right ways, that wives should as a matter of course submit silently to their husbands, that youth should as a matter of course submit to age. The play, in short, stays safely within the world of comedy, and never crosses disturbingly into the world of satire; it never lets us feel (as Jonson's comedies, for all their apparently clear moral contrasts, so often do let us feel) the disturbance of a moral cross-current or paradox; it exerts little pressure on our thought; it never surprises us with its ideas, but only with the mechanics of its narrative. It is the product of a secure, pre-Civil War society; a generation later, it was already to look old-fashioned: 'much mirth, but no great matter else' was Pepys's comment upon seeing the play revived in

1661.[1] The comedy of the 1660s was to be altogether less comfortable and easy in its mood. And yet as Swinburne remarked,[2] Brome's comedy has the peculiar interest of lying midway between the comedy of Jonson and the comedy of Wycherley. It is to Wycherley's most difficult play that we must now turn; to a play which, like *The Antipodes*, contrasts the ways of the Old World with those of the New, establishing a moral polarity by means of geographical reference.

[1] *The Diary of Samuel Pepys*, ed. H. B. Wheatley (London, 1928), 8 vols., ii. 83.

[2] *The Complete Works of A. C. Swinburne*, ed. Sir Edmund Gosse and T. J. Wise (London, 1926), xii. 334.

CHAPTER FIVE

'Tables Turned': *The Plain Dealer*

Th' extreams of *Glory*, and of *Shame*,
Like *East* and *West*, become the same.
Hudibras, II. i. 271–2.

'H E was universally admir'd, and reckon'd in the first Rank
of Comic Poets, and the next excellent to Ben. *Johnson*',
wrote Charles Gildon in his short *Life of William Wycherley
Esq.*, in 1718, adding that his plays were 'so excellent in
their Kind, that they will be admir'd and valu'd as long as
our Language is understood'. The prophecy was rash. Of
Wycherley's four plays, only *The Country Wife* continues to
enjoy a theatrical life and (to use the phrase in a limited
sense) a modest reputation. That no one today is likely to
want to stage *Love in a Wood* or *The Gentleman Dancing-Master*
is hardly a matter for surprise or regret. The eclipse of
The Plain Dealer, however, is a good deal more interesting.
It was *The Plain Dealer*, not *The Country Wife*, which many
of Wycherley's most discerning friends and contemporaries
thought his best play; it was to *The Plain Dealer* that
Dryden was referring in his prefatory essay to *The State of
Innocence* when he said that Wycherley had 'obliged all
honest and virtuous men, and enrich'd our stage by one of
the most bold, most general, and most useful satires, which
has ever been presented on the English theatre'.[1] If the
play seldom receives a tribute of that kind today, the reason
would seem to be that it offers a central interpretative
difficulty which apparently did not greatly worry Wycherley's

---

[1] *Essays*, ed. W. P. Ker (Oxford, 1900), i. 182.

contemporaries.[1] The difficulty is sometimes expressed as one of *kind*: is *The Plain Dealer* to be formally regarded as a satire, a romantic comedy, a tragi-comedy, a re-write of Molière, a comedy of manners, or what? Modern readers have shown more distress over the play's habit of melting from one kind into another than did the neo-classical Dryden, who simply remarked on Wycherley's skill in joining humour with satire. The question of the play's dramatic kind leads, however, to another question which is at once more central and more teasing: is Manly the romantic hero of the play, or its comic gull? is he partly the object, or wholly the agent, of this bold, general, and useful satire?

Macaulay, echoing Leigh Hunt, had no doubt that Manly's fierceness, misanthropy, and curious moral imbalance were qualities shared by Wycherley himself.[2] Modern reactions against Macaulay's reading of *The Plain Dealer* have been very much along the same lines as the reactions against Thackeray's reading of *Gulliver's Travels*, and the fine tools of rhetorical and formal analysis have been used to separate Manly from Wycherley, and Gulliver from Swift. The most subtle and extended of such analyses of the dramatist's work—the analysis from which any new examination of Wycherley must now begin—is Rose Zimbardo's recent book, *Wycherley's Drama: A Link in the Development of English Satire*.[3] Mrs. Zimbardo's argument (to condense it briefly) is that in *The Plain Dealer* Wycherley draws on traditions of both classical and native satire; Manly is the familiar figure of the satyr who poses as satirist, the railer who is infected with the vices against which he

---

[1] Not, at any rate, his more distinguished contemporaries. Dennis reports that the decisive lead given by such men as Buckingham, Rochester, Dorset, Mulgrave, Denham, and Waller finally won the support of audiences which were initially hesitant about the play. See *The Critical Works of John Dennis*, ed. E. N. Hooker (Baltimore, 1943), ii. 277.

[2] *Works* (1906–8), i. 428–30.   [3] New Haven, 1965.

rails. The action of the play, in this view, is the progressive exposure of Manly's hypocrisy, which we watch not with sympathy but with critical detachment; by the end of the play Manly has deserted whatever standards he once professed, and Freeman is unchallenged in his view that Manly has reconciled himself to the world merely out of self-interest. At the beginning of the book Mrs. Zimbardo places, without comment, a brief extract from Lansdowne's *A Character of Mr. Wycherley and his Writings* (1701) which testifies to the dramatist's personal mildness and compassion. The separation between the civilized Wycherley and the shaggy, cloven-hoofed Manly is complete.

The great attraction of an argument of this kind is that it stabilizes a play which seems alarmingly wanton in its various emotional appeals. Yet for a number of reasons the argument that Manly is a mere satyr, like other recent arguments that he is a mere malcontent, psychopath, or comic dupe, remains a good deal less than satisfying. One may begin with the minor and apparently external matter of biographical evidence. It is good to have Macaulayism countered by the cool and measured testimony of Lansdowne; yet before that testimony is used (however obliquely) to imply a total divorce between Wycherley and Manly, it is worth recalling how Lansdowne's *Character* concludes:

In Mr. Wycherley every thing is Masculine . . . like your Heroes of Antiquity, he charges in Iron, and seems to despise all Ornament, but intrinsick Merit: And like those Heroes has therefore added another Name to his own, and by the unanimous Consent of his Contemporaries, is distinguish'd by the just Appellation of Manly *Wycherley*.

Had Rochester, Dennis, Dryden, Congreve, and Pope misunderstood their friend's play, or were they being ironical, when they spoke of him as 'the Plain Dealer' and as 'manly Wycherley'? Are there ironical implications (and if so, why?) in Wycherley's own use of 'the Plain Dealer' as a name for himself (signing himself thus, for instance, in the Preface to the *Miscellany Poems* of 1704)? Why should Wycherley have actually encouraged an identification between himself and a goatish satyr? Wycherley later dedicated *The Plain Dealer* 'To My Lady B—' (Mother Bennett, the bawd), signing the Dedication 'The Plain Dealer'; the urbanely ironical voice of the Dedication, though it is lighter, on the whole, than that of Manly, frequently gathers his tone, and it attacks, as Manly attacks, the hypocrisy of women. Author and character are, in fact, deliberately confused here; and that confusion deepens in the Prologue. Here Manly speaks of himself as 'rough', and of the author as 'coarse' (in the critique of *The Country Wife* in the second act of *The Plain Dealer* Novel refers to the author again as a 'surly fool'); the role of Manly as author's spokesman is unequivocal: 'Our scribbler therefore bluntly bid me say. . . .'

Nor, as the play proceeds, is it easy to keep Manly neatly in his place as gull or satyr. It is scarcely credible, for instance, that we are meant to question Fidelia's sincerity when in the first act she praises Manly to his face: 'Fame, the old liar, is believed when she speaks wonders of you: you cannot be flattered, sir, your merit is unspeakable' (I. i). Like Olivia's crudely explicit confessions ('I have used him so scurvily, his great spirit will ne'er return to reason it farther with me': IV. ii) such a remark seems all too clearly designed to encourage the audience not to lose trust. Norman Holland argues that Manly should be seen as a comic dupe, and that Eliza and Freeman represent a sane middle way which is contrasted favourably with Manly's extremism.[1] But Freeman is simply a cheerful trickster,

[1] Norman Holland, *The First Modern Comedies* (Bloomington and London, 1959), Ch. 10.

certainly no Philintes; and Eliza is a marginal character who is really no more than a foil to Olivia; Wycherley has taken so little trouble over her that he allows her to contradict herself utterly (about Lord Plausible, ii. i) within a matter of moments. The real rock upon which such theories as Mr. Holland's and Mrs. Zimbardo's split, however, is the play's ending. If Manly is simply a dupe or railing malcontent, one would expect him to be finally exposed ridiculed, and allowed to make—as Vernish does—a final, 'dogged', exit. Notoriously, Manly does not make the lone haughty exit at the end of the play that is made by Alceste, Morose, Jaques, and Malvolio. In this curiously inside-out version of *Twelfth Night*, that exit is made by Olivia:

> *Widow Blackacre.* I'll follow the law for you.
> *Olivia.* And I my revenge.   [Exit

Manly is rewarded by Fidelia's love and fortune, and abandons his plan 'to go live and bask himself on the sunny side of the globe'. Comedy has few more certain ways of securing our final sympathies for a character (however nasty he may have been; even a Bertram and an Angelo) than such an ending. That such rewards as these seldom occur in real life had been acknowledged as early as the play's Prologue:

> And where else, but on stages, do we see
> Truth pleasing, or rewarded honesty?

But there is no suggestion that Manly does not deserve these rewards.

The real trouble with an approach as decisive as Mrs. Zimbardo's is that it reduces Manly from a richly enigmatic figure to one as simple as Heartwell in *The Old Bachelor*, and so denies the play its central power of paradox, of shifting and re-shifting our sympathies, of allowing us to see all that is self-contradictory and self-defeating in Manly at the same time that it exacts admiration for him. Empson's

phrase about the blind Samson is very much to the point.[1]
A confident judgement that Shakespeare's Timon is simply
a malcontent (or simply a psychological case, or a type of
Christ) misses the real force of that play, which is to arouse
conflicting feelings as to whether Timon is childish, criminal, or divine, or indeed all these things at once. A
confident judgement that Swift stands at an amused, ironic
distance from Gulliver throughout the whole of the fourth
book of *Gulliver's Travels*, that Gulliver is totally deluded
in his admiration of the Houyhnhnms, may clarify the work
only at the expense of that dubiety, that power of vexation,
which Swift seems to have been at pains to create. The
same kind of confidence makes *The Plain Dealer* a tidier,
but also a tamer play. *The Plain Dealer* is in fact a play that is
difficult because of its strong feeling of contradictoriness.
This contradictoriness seems to me to be deliberate and (for
the most part) controlled, the source of the play's energy
and brilliance.

Wycherley's chief predilection, and it is far more than a
verbal habit, is for pun, oxymoron, paradox, and identification of things which at first appear to be opposites. The
world of *The Plain Dealer* is like the characteristic world of
Jonson, one in which 'things daily fall; wits grow downe-
ward, and *Eloquence* growes back-ward' (*Discoveries*, 921–2);
a mirror world, where sense can only be made by turning
things back-to-front:

... for all wise observers understand us now-a-days, as they do
dreams, almanacs, and Dutch gazettes, by the contrary: and a
man no more believes a woman, when she says she has an aversion
for him, than when she says she'll cry out.   (II. i)

> For plays, like women, by the world are thought,
> When you speak kindly of 'em, very naught.
>   (Epilogue)

[1] William Empson, *The Structure of Complex Words* (London, 1952), p. 193.

Olivia's hypocrisy is only one example (and that probably
the least subtle) of this back-to-frontness. It is a play in
which actions and words seldom mean what they seem to
signify. Freeman talks love to Widow Blackacre when he
is simply after her cash; Widow Blackacre uses the language
of sexual intrigue (e.g. v. iii) to discuss matters of business;
Fidelia, the most devoted and courageous character of the
play, is continually taken to be a weak lover and a coward;
Manly kicks his sailors though he is affectionate and
generous towards them. 'Most men', as Harcourt remarks
in *The Country Wife*, 'are the contraries to that they would
seem.' The most deceptive of all actions in the play is a
loving embrace. In the Dedication to the play the Plain
Dealer discusses female critics who insist on turning an
author's words to their opposite, and indecent meanings,
and whose contrariness is such that 'nothing is secure from
the power of their imaginations, no, not their husbands,
whom they cuckold with themselves, by thinking of other
men; and so make the lawful matrimonial embraces adultery,
wrong husbands and poets in thought and word, to keep
their own reputations'. *Conjugal Lewdness; or Matrimonial
Whoredom*, was how Defoe was later to describe this mental
crime in a pair of indignant oxymorons.[1] Throughout the
play the idea is repeated in different ways: people embrace
for any reason but love. 'For such as you,' says Manly to
Plausible in the first scene of the play, 'like common whores
and pickpockets, are only dangerous to those you embrace.'
'Could you think I was a friend to all those I hugged . . .?'
asks Freeman in the same scene; and Manly declares he
'would give fawning slaves the lie whilst they embrace or
commend me'. Mistaken embraces keep occurring; Manly
twice embraces Vernish (v. ii) not realizing that his friend

[1] Cf. Marston, *The Malcontent*, i. i. 161–7; Rochester, 'A Satyr Against
Mankind', lines 204–5; Jonson, Epigram xxvi; Seneca, *De Constantia*, ii. vii. 4.

has betrayed him; Olivia, meeting with Fidelia, 'threw her twisting arms about my neck, and smothered me with a thousand tasteless kisses' (IV. i), not realizing Fidelia to be a girl; arranging to meet her again in the darkened house, she mistakenly embraces and kisses her husband who has unexpectedly returned (IV. ii); later in the same scene she sleeps with Manly, taking him for Fidelia, though she has sworn that she would 'sooner take a bedfellow out of a hospital, and diseases into her arms' (IV. i): in the final moments of the play she is revealed, by the sudden entry of sailors bearing torches, to be once more mistakenly in Manly's arms. Hypocrisy—heart not going with hand —is punished in kind by the traditional confusions of comedy.

Such confusions and reversals as these may guide us to the play's central structural device, which might be described by the old rhetorical term which we met in chapter one: *inversion*, or the turning of a speaker's accusation back upon himself. Again, the precedent of Jonson, in, say, *Bartholomew Fair* comes strongly to mind. Before coming to the most difficult case of inversion in *The Plain Dealer*, that involving Manly, we may begin with one or two simpler and more obvious examples of the play's chief structural characteristic. Take, for instance, Vernish's unexpected home-coming in the fourth act which interrupts Olivia's rendezvous with Fidelia. Olivia flees; Fidelia is left alone with Vernish, whose reactions are those of the outraged husband seeking satisfaction for his honour. Fidelia ('I'll satisfy you, sir') reveals that she is a woman. In the words of the stage direction, Vernish *pulls off her peruke and feels her breasts*. The action is as ambiguous as the pickpocket's embrace; it serves at once to ensure Vernish that his 'honour' as a husband is safe (he can't have been cuckolded after all), and to put at risk the honour of Fidelia: Vernish now wants 'satisfaction' of a different kind, the ease with which he switches from the role of outraged husband to gleeful seducer immediately neutralizing any positive sense which his talk of 'honour' might have had. 'Well, *I'm glad to find the tables turned*; my wife is in more danger of cuckolding than I was': like the title of the play,[1] Vernish's phrase is drawn from gaming (the notion is that of a table set with cards or chess pieces being reversed in mid game), and may serve to describe the play's over-all structural method.

Almost any Restoration dramatist might have brought about that comic moment, but Wycherley does more, trans- forming, as Jonson does, the simple stage jokes about sexual identity into more intricate themes. We may watch how he does this first in *The Country Wife*. Horner, a virile philan- derer, pretends to be his opposite, an impotent misogynist. This 'no man' (as he is called) meets Margery Pinchwife, who has been disguised by her anxious husband as a boy; doubly disguised, they kiss, Margery manfully protesting 'What do you kiss me for? I am no woman' (III. ii). It is like Morose's confession at the end of *Epicoene*, 'I am no man, ladies', which comes fractionally before the disclosure that his wife is no lady; but Wycherley, like Jonson, screws the paradox further. Horner, a mere 'sign of a man', declares himself thankful that he is now free to dedicate himself to 'manly pleasures' (I. i), the whole joke of the play being that the word 'manly' includes the two contra- dictory senses of sexual abstinence and sexual indulgence. The paradox turns again in the 'china' scene, where Horner is actually temporarily reduced to that state of sexual incapacity to which he had earlier pretended. In this dizzy world, the whole notion of manliness is subjected to

[1] Charles Cotton, *The Compleat Gamester* (London, 1674), p. 142: '*A Game called* Plain-dealing'.

continual ironic reversals, so that its exact meaning is always in doubt:

> *Horner.* You have found me a true man, I'm sure. [*Aside* to Lady Fidget.
> *Lady Fidget.* Not every way. [*Aside* to Horner.   (v. iv)

In *The Plain Dealer* this linguistic uncertainty gathers implications at once more complex and more obviously moral, the question 'What is manliness?' now being seriously related to the validity of different possible attitudes to life. In the course of the play the name 'Manly' takes on a variety of senses, each of which is later contradicted or found to be true only in a paradoxical sense; yet the original senses are never quite dislodged. Manly is manly, for instance, because he is virile, unlike Oldfox, Plausible, and Novel, who 'are in all things so like women' (II. i). Widow Blackacre's attack on Oldfox concentrates on his sexual incompetence—'impotent, fumbling, frigid nincompoop' (II. i)—and Oldfox's attempted 'rape' of the widow turns out to be merely an attempt to read her his bad verses ('it shall be through the ear, lady, the ear only, with my well-penned acrostics'), even this being frustrated (v. iii). Such men are characterized by Manly as 'gaudy fluttering parrots of the town, apes and echoes of men only' (I. i). But Manly's manliness gets him nowhere; Olivia actually prefers apes and echoes of men, and Freeman ironically throws Manly's phrase back in his teeth in the second act. When in v. iv Manly declares that Olivia's impudence is almost enough to 'make revenge itself impotent', the adjective is carefully chosen. Again, Manly is manly because of his courage; but learning of Olivia's treachery he declares he 'could outrail a bilked whore, or a kicked coward' (II. i); Olivia compares Manly's cunning to 'the coward's sword, by which he is oftener worsted than defended' (IV. ii). The connotations of the name turn continually to an ironical sense. Manly is manly because he is fully adult and independent, unlike Jerry Blackacre, whose 'curmudgeonly mother won't allow me wherewithal to be a man of myself with' (III. i); yet Manly is entirely dependent upon the trust and goodwill first of one girl and then of another. Manly is manly because he is human, in contrast to the men of the town who are parrots, apes, chattering baboons, spaniels, men such as Novel who considers a monkey to be 'a wit' (V. ii). But looked at from the viewpoint of Olivia, Manly is a sea-monster (IV. i) and worse:

Olivia. Surly, untractable, snarling brute! He! a mastiff dog were as fit a thing to make a gallant of.
Manly. Ay, a goat, or monkey, were fitter for thee. [*Aside.*
Fidelia. I must confess, for my part, though my rival, I cannot but say he has a manly handsomeness in's face and mien.
Olivia. So has a Saracen in the sign.

And Manly himself encourages the paradox by preferring the honest beastliness of uncivilized man: 'I rather choose to go where honest, downright barbarity is professed, where men devour one another like generous hungry lions and tigers, not like crocodiles; where they think the devil white, of our complexion; and I am already so far an Indian' (I. i). That the necessary and regular laws of animal life are preferable to the wanton and arbitrary ones of mankind is a common enough proposition in seventeenth-century primitivist philosophy and satire,[1] finding its classic

---

[1] George Boas, *The Happy Beast in French Thought of the Seventeenth Century* (Baltimore, 1933). Cf. Wycherley's poem '*Upon the Impertinence of* Knowledge, *the Unreasonableness of* Reason, *and the Brutality of* Humanity; *proving the Animal Life the most Reasonable Life, since the most Natural, and most Innocent*', in *The Complete Works of William Wycherley*, ed. Montague Summers (London, 1924), iii. 149-54.

statement in Boileau's eighth satire and in Rochester's 'A Satyr Against Mankind':

> Which is the basest *Creature, Man,* or *Beast*?
> *Birds,* feed on *Birds, Beasts,* on each other prey,
> But Savage *Man* alone, does *Man,* betray:
> Prest by necessity, they Kill for Food,
> *Man,* undoes *Man,* to do himself no good.
> With Teeth, and Claws by Nature arm'd they hunt,
> Natures allowances, to supply their want.
> But *Man,* with smiles, embraces, Friendships, praise,
> Unhumanely his Fellows life betrays.   (128–36)

But the possibility of such a philosophy recoiling upon its proponent could scarcely be more delicately suggested than by calling the proponent *Manly*. Beneath the general, admiring connotations of the name gather more subversive suggestions.

When Manly proposes to Fidelia that he will go along with her to Olivia 'and act love, whilst you shall talk it only' (IV. i) another equation of opposites has been made; Manly's tactics are now those of Olivia; words no longer go with deeds, the language of love conceals motives of revenge; Manly's is now the Judas kiss. Even Manly's own motives are not clear, oscillating violently between lust and hatred: 'Her love!—a whore's, a witch's love!—But what, did she not kiss well, sir?—I'm sure I thought her lips—but I must not think of 'em more—but yet they are such I could still kiss—grow to—and then tear off with my teeth, grind 'em into mammocks, and spit 'em into her cuckold's face.' It is these emotional oscillations which constantly tear the play from one dramatic kind to another, from the world of *Twelfth Night* to that of *Othello*: 'I will chop her into messes: cuckold me?' 'Manly'? 'Honourable'? 'Revenge'? The words are all held up for ironic scrutiny, Manly's moral inconsistency being discreetly indicated by Fidelia all the while: 'Think of your honour, sir: love!—'; ' 'Tis a strange revenge'; 'you are your own enemy'. The feeling which the scene generates is one of handy-dandy, of continual reversibility; but though we are certainly intended to see Manly's reversal as morally reprehensible, we are also invited to see it as pardonable in a way that Olivia's hypocrisy is not, the good senses of manliness finally cancelling out the ironical ones.

Yet *The Plain Dealer* has a curious feeling of weight-lessness about it. Another of the play's complex words, Norman Holland suggests (pp. 109 ff.), is *world*. The word is indeed used by different characters throughout the play in different senses: there is the world of society to which Olivia professes an aversion, and to which she fears secrets will leak; there is the world of law-abiding citizens who are troubled by Widow Blackacre's litigation (i. i); the world of worldly shrewdness in which Vernish is schooled (ii. i) and in which he will always be tolerated (v. iv). But the most important contrast is that between, on the one hand, the sensible but imaginatively inert world which Freeman follows ('against your particular notions, I have the practice of the whole world': i. i) and from which he judges Manly ('the world thinks you a mad man, a brutal'), and on the other hand 'the sunny side of the globe' (i. i), and 'the Indian world' (v. iv), which Manly holds of value, and to which he wants to return. Each world stands judged in the eyes of the other. Which world provides the standards by which we, the audience, should make our judgement?

The geographical image no longer provides an unambiguous guide for us here, as it does in Brome's *Antipodes*, or in such a play as Richard Cumberland's *The West Indian* (1771), where the New World—'that warm sunny region, where naked nature walks without disguise'—is sentimentally praised at the expense of the Old—'this cold contriving artificial country' (IV. x). In *The Plain Dealer* the two worlds weigh more evenly in the balance; the Indian world, though it is finally rejected, has value to the end; the London world is 'this ill world of ours still', even though it is the one for which Manly finally settles. The Indian world still has its somewhat incredible air of pastoral innocence ('one keeps shifting to the memory of accounts of actual savages', says Empson, '—how did he suppose that this tribe kept itself going?'), the London world is still intractable and unredeemed. By the standards of which world do we judge Manly? In the Prologue the Plain Dealer has little doubt that a wordly audience will pass a worldly judgement, but the possibility of different ways of looking at the situation is not excluded:

> I, only, act a part like none of you,
> And yet *you'll say*, it is a fool's part too. [my italics]

It is not likely, however, that a contemporary audience would have seen Manly simply as a pastoral type. The play has the real and contemporary setting of the Dutch Wars (it is thought that Wycherley himself took part in the famous naval victory over Opdam in 1665).[1] One of the play's first contrasts, pointed up by Manly's sailors in the first scene, is between Manly, who serves his country with honour in the wars, and Lord Plausible, contemptuously referred to as 'one of those that get the king's commissions for hulls to sell a king's ship, when a brave fellow has fought her almost to a standstill'. Manly, who captains a convoy escorting merchant ships to India and back, is uncompromising in his sense of duty, not allowing his men to do their own business on the side, quickly returning his ships to the docks and his casualties to the hospital. Yet

---

[1] *Works*, ed. Summers, Introduction, p. 17.

on the fleet's return to England, Manly's honour has driven him to sink his own ship; his reason is not simply to prevent her falling into the hands of the Dutch, but to prevent her falling into the hands of such men as Plausible. It is as futile and as damaging to the national interest to sink ships as to acquire them for profitable resale; between Manly and Plausible there is not much to choose; honour and dishonour are equally disastrous. And in sinking his own ship Manly has sunk his own fortune of five or six thousand pounds; such honour is suicidal.

The scenes with Widow Blackacre and the lawyers of Westminster Hall are often taken to be structurally irrelevant; John Wain, for instance, takes them to be robust Shakespearian interludes that do something towards redeeming a play that is generally pretty nasty.[1] The legal scenes of *The Plain Dealer* are in fact structurally central, the 'civil' ways of Westminster, based on the code of law, being at first contrasted and later paradoxically equated with the 'rough' ways of the sea, based on the code of revenge (Bacon's 'kind of wild justice'). The sense of equally distributed weight might almost be seen in Wycherley's own life; he was not only sailor but also lawyer, as he reminds the 'Squires of the long robe' in the Epilogue:

> He has a just right in abusing you
> Because he is a Brother-Templar too.

The lawyers of the play wear black robes (Manly puns on this when he calls them a 'numerous black-guard'), the sailors wear red breeches, the contrast between the two ways of life being strongly marked in stage terms; when Jerry decides to follow in Freeman's path, leaving the law for the sea, he changes from black to red. A characteristic uncertainty hangs around the word *law*. When Widow

[1] *Preliminary Essays* (London, 1957), pp. 1-35.

Blackacre calls Manly a 'lawless companion' (I. i) the force of the adjective is neutralized, indeed put into reverse, by what we know about lawyers and the law, the effect being the same as the law-crazed Trouble-all's condemnation of the lawlessness of Bartholomew Fair in the name of Justice Overdo. 'Would you have a man speak truth to his ruin?' Freeman asks Manly in the first scene, framing a central question of the play. 'You are severer than the law, which requires no man to swear against himself.' We are teased by an almost Marlovian uncertainty as to whether Manly breaks laws like a god or a criminal. By a curious process of levelling, those utterly opposed characters, Manly and Widow Blackacre, are shown paradoxically to resemble one another. Each strives, in a different way (railing, litigation) to achieve independence; the widow's stance, like Manly's, is that of *unus contra mundum*, 'at law and difference with all the world' (I. i; Freeman speaking); each fanatically follows a code of life to the point of self-ruin: Widow Blackacre's 'lawyers, attorneys, and solicitors, have fifteen hundred pounds a year, whilst she is contented to be poor, to make other people so' (I. i)—the same mentality which brings Manly to sink his own ship and fortune. The paradoxes of the situation find their outlet in oxymoron: a lawyer is 'a most barbarous civil rogue' (III. i).

The constant possibilities of table-turning are best noticed in the exposure scene of v. iv. The real question about this scene is who is exposing whom? The scene takes place in darkness (like so many of Wycherley's scenes) in the lodgings of Olivia, who is expecting another meeting with Fidelia. Two different exposures have been planned from two different directions; Olivia is to be the victim of each, but not the only victim. The first exposure has been planned by Manly, who has brought with him to the house a crowd of witnesses who will burst in at an appropriate moment and catch Olivia in the midst of her supposed adultery. The second exposure has been planned by Vernish, who is trying to discover what his wife is up to. Fidelia enters the darkened house, 'followed softly by Manly'. It is difficult to forget that shortly before this Manly, now so full of righteousness, entered Olivia's house in order to sleep with Olivia; that Olivia's only technical infidelity (so far as we know) has actually been with Manly himself. Vernish arrives, breaks down the door, there is a fight in the dark. In the middle of the fight Manly's witnesses enter, *lighted by two Sailors with torches*, to reveal—what? Olivia discovers that the man to whom she gave her money and jewels in the dark, whom she now holds in her arms, and with whom she must have slept, is Manly; by strict justice Manly may be guilty both of conversion and rape, but Olivia is silenced by consciousness of her own guilt by the standards of wild justice, by which both the money and she herself are Manly's. Comic justice and wild justice overturn legal justice; the whirligig of time brings in his revenges. Vernish next discovers the identity of the man who has cuckolded him: Manly. Vernish too is silenced by his consciousness of having taken Olivia from Manly in the first place. And at the same time that Olivia's double-dealing is exposed, so too is the fact that Fidelia is a woman. Embarrassment is distributed pretty equally in all directions at once, touching even Manly.

Why does Wycherley, having so consistently allowed us to see Manly's moral and physical vulnerability, nevertheless keep him always on a tether of sympathy, and draw him in finally for such handsome rewards? The usual answers, that Wycherley was either morally very obtuse or technically very clumsy, seem inappropriate to a play in which (in most other respects (moral and formal questions have been so obviously pondered. The accusation that Wycherley wrote in tolerant collusion with the worst tastes of his audiences (an accusation not confined to Meredith and the nineteenth-century critics) seems equally strange: no English dramatist except Jonson (to whom, once again, one turns instinctively for comparison) has conveyed so consistently in his plays the feeling that the satirical fire is not safely contained within the area of the stage, but that it touches the motives, consciences, and reactions of the audience themselves. Repeatedly in his prologues, epilogues, and such hall-of-mirrors devices as the critique of *The Country Wife*, Wycherley makes the point that his audiences are as vulnerable as the characters at whom they laugh: 'But why shouldst thou be afraid of being in a play, who expose yourself every day in the play-houses, and at public places? . . . 'Tis but being on the stage, instead of standing on a bench in the pit' (*The Country Wife*, III. ii). Even the security of the playwright's own position ('the surly fool') is not free from ironic scrutiny. The ironic reversals that are sprung on Manly are ones that, unless he moves delicately, may spring too on Wycherley.

Different authors may have different motives in their use of the dramatic type of the railer. They may create such a figure in order to show that railing is idle and ill-advised, as is Molière's way with Alceste, and Shakespeare's, perhaps, with Jaques. On the other hand, they may want to show, not as a cautionary tale, but with amusement and sympathy (for the problem is very near to that of the satirical dramatist himself) how very difficult it is to be a satirist, and yet how necessary it is, things being what they are, that the satirist continues to exist. *The Plain Dealer* treats in a complex, ironical, and basically sympathetic way the problem of the hazards which beset a satirist. It is difficult to be a satirist at a time when 'railing now is so common, that 'tis no more malice, but the fashion' (ii. i), when 'raillery' or 'rallying' is practised by everyone from Major Oldfox ('the way of all such sober persons as myself, when they have a mind to publish their disgust to the times' : iv. i) and Novel ('for railing is satire, you know; and roaring and making a noise, humour': v. ii) to Olivia, Widow Blackacre, and the lawyers of Westminster; when even the audience are likely to 'rail' against the very play they are watching (Prologue). It is difficult, too, to be a satirist when one is betrayed by false libels, false friends, false appearances, even by one's own false feelings, which permit the shafts to come hurtling back again in the direction from which they have been sent.

Even an explanation of the play along these lines does not, however, remove its puzzling feeling of instability; an instability that evidently disturbed those early audiences, and does something to explain the play's present theatrical neglect. The play's most obvious weaknesses—to do no more than note them—are two. First, Wycherley's wit, as Wilson Knight has said of Shaw's,[1] is suicidal; he overplays his ambiguities, and when the time has come for the game to end cannot firmly enough exclude the suggestion that the tables may easily turn again. Secondly, although Manly begs Fidelia's pardon for having been a bit brusque with her, not knowing she was a girl, and although he tells us in the closing lines that he has tempered his scepticism with a new wisdom about the possible goodness of men and women, there is still that mysterious, sublime lack of self-awareness of Manly, that surprising failure to say anything about the riskiness or moral culpability of the tactics he has adopted. No doubt this lack of self-awareness in Manly will continue to be taken by some readers as a lack of moral awareness in Wycherley himself; such a judgement is, I

[1] *The Golden Labyrinth* (London, 1965), p. 351.

think, certainly wrong but at least understandable. Intricate and assured though the play is for the most part, its faults are, I think, basically technical (not moral) in their nature. Wycherley's brilliance is altogether narrower, and less controlled than that of Jonson; but that Gildon's contemporaries should have grouped the two men together is both illuminating and just.

CHAPTER SIX

'Dear Liberty': *The Way of the World*

It were perhaps, the Work of a long Life to make one
Comedy true in all its Parts . . .
CONGREVE to DENNIS, 10 July 1695.[1]

T H E first performance of *The Way of the World* in March
1700 was coolly received, and the play was generally
reckoned to be something of a disappointment. Congreve,
aged 30, stopped writing for the stage; his dramatic career
had spanned a mere seven years. Though he lived on until
1729, enjoying from a remarkably youthful age the eminence
of a literary elder statesman, Congreve was not to see this
initial verdict on *The Way of the World* reversed; until the
1720s, indeed, the play was only very occasionally performed, and throughout the century it was generally
reckoned to be inferior to Congreve's earlier comedies,
Love for Love and *The Old Bachelor*. Modern critics, shaking
their heads over these sad and now familiar facts of stage
history, have done their lavish best to compensate for the
ignorance of their ancestors. In recent years the play's
reputation has spectacularly grown: Bonamy Dobrée,
Kathleen Lynch, Virginia Woolf, and Paul and Miriam
Mueschke (to name only a few) have inspected it with
praise and love. Today the play is freely described as a
masterpiece, as the apotheosis of the English comic genius.
Norman Holland, approvingly quoting Lytton Strachey's
remark that *The Way of the World* is 'among the most
wonderful and glorious creations of the human mind',
compares the play to the late work of Shakespeare and of

[1] *William Congreve: Letters and Documents*, ed. John C. Hodges (London,
1964), p. 184.

Beethoven. No other comedy in English stage history has enjoyed so spectacular a reversal of its fortunes.[1]

While it is good to see the play's qualities so warmly appreciated, the terms in which the piece has been praised may nevertheless strike one as somewhat odd. Congreve was hardly like the mature Shakespeare when he wrote *The Way of the World*, nor was he yet as accomplished as the mature Ben Jonson. It was a matter not only of years but also of confidence. *The Way of the World* was written in the immediate aftermath of Jeremy Collier's *Short View*, at a time when replies and counter-replies were still coming very freely from the presses.[2] It is clear enough from the tone of Congreve's *Amendments of Mr. Collier's False and Imperfect Citations* (1698) that he had been seriously distressed by Collier's blunt objections to his plays, and equally clear from Congreve's arguments that he was not perfectly at ease with the formidable moral and aesthetic questions which the Collier debate had suddenly brought into prominence. In writing *The Way of the World* in 1699 (the year of Collier's *A Defence of the Short View . . . Being a Reply to Mr. Congreve's Amendments &c.*), Congreve seems to have made a quite deliberate attempt to trump Collier's criticisms by producing a new kind of comedy which—to speak in Addisonian terms—would join wit with virtue. Paul and Miriam Mueschke's long, subtle, and rewarding essay on the play analyses the way in which Congreve attempted to modify his early techniques in order to give *The Way of the World* a clear yet intricate moral design.

---

[1] Emmett L. Avery, *Congreve's Plays on the Eighteenth-Century Stage* (New York, 1951), p. 155; Bonamy Dobrée, *Restoration Comedy, 1660–1720* (London, 1924), Ch. VIII; Kathleen M. Lynch, *The Social Mode of Restoration Comedy* (New York, 1926), Ch. VII; Paul and Miriam Mueschke, *A New View of Congreve's 'The Way of the World'* (Ann Arbor, 1958); Norman N. Holland, *The First Modern Comedies* (Bloomington and London, 1959), Ch. 15.

[2] Joseph Wood Krutch, *Comedy and Conscience After the Restoration* (New York, 1961), pp. 267–70.

The Mueschkes' conclusion, that Congreve was brilliantly successful in this attempt, has been very favourably received by later commentators. Congreve's last play is certainly in many respects an astonishing work, graceful, supple, and complex. And yet it is a play in which, I think, one can also sense the presence of certain cracks and strains, in both the narrative and moral design; and in which one can sense, too, a curious over-all distribution of weight. Collier no doubt must take his share of the blame for this. Yet in 1699 Congreve was still a young, and, to an extent, experimental, playwright, and it is not really surprising that we should find him at times worsted by a variety of technical problems. In admiring the peculiar achievement of *The Way of the World* we may do well, first, to keep constantly in mind certain criticisms which have been made since the play's first performance, often with most precision by eighteenth-century commentators; and, secondly, to compare the play with that of the mature work of the dramatist by whom Congreve was probably most deeply influenced, Ben Jonson.

The first and traditional difficulty that the play presents is in the matter of plot. There is a well-known letter from Lady Marow to a friend in the country describing the play after its first performance: 'Congreve's new play doth not answer expectation, there being no plot in it but many witty things to ridicule the Chocolate House, and the fantastical part of the world.'[1] *No plot*: the notion is as curious as T. S. Eliot's notion that Ben Jonson's skill lay in 'doing without a plot'; in each case, one suspects, the comment means that the narrative-line is so energetic and busy that it actually obscures itself with incidental detail. Yet Jonson's plots are in fact seldom vexatiously

[1] Historical MSS. Commission, *Dartmouth*, iii. 145; cited in John C. Hodges, *William Congreve the Man* (New York and London, 1941), p. 68.

demanding in the theatre, for the main lines of action are almost always clear and simple. With Congreve, the case is otherwise. *The Way of the World* deserves and rewards constant re-reading, and one's pleasure is enhanced at each reading (or seeing) by the discovery of new dimensions and corners of the plot. And yet it is fair to say that this intricacy cannot be fully grasped by an unprepared audience; the play is top-heavy in hints, nuances, oblique clues, complications. The question is a simple one of theatrical tolerance. One of Shakespeare's gifts is his unerring calculation of the extent to which the unsophisticated members of his audience can tolerate narrative surprise; Coleridge noted as the first of his 'Characteristics of Shakespeare' that his plays encouraged 'Expectation in preference to surprize'.[1] In, say, *All's Well that Ends Well* the early scenes of the play reiterate constantly for us the narrative situation upon which the play has opened, without ever appearing repetitive or condescending or even particularly direct in their conveyance of this information. This might be described as theatrical good manners. Jonson's narrative method, on the other hand, is more covert and subtle, and has little of the Shakespearian openness about it: it challenges our wits. When the method outruns itself, as in *The New Inn*, the result tends to be frankly ludicrous. It is a narrative method which, unlike Shakespeare's, was to influence the eighteenth-century novel; and Congreve, an obvious follower of the method, seems to stand midway on a line which runs from Jonson to Fielding. The work which seems the natural successor to *The Way of the World* is in fact *Tom Jones*; Fielding was as saturated in Congreve's dramatic techniques as Congreve had been in Jonson's. Fielding's plot, unlike Congreve's, always seems to be

[1] S. T. Coleridge, *Shakespearean Criticism*, ed. T. M. Raysor (London and New York, 1960), i. 199.

under perfect, though not too conspicuous, control. The plot of *Tom Jones* is enjoyable for a number of reasons: because its threads help bind together such an extensive and apparently sprawling narrative; because it seems legitimate that a novelist should tuck away some of his important clues (such as those concerning Lawyer Dowling) in the less obvious corners of his work; and because the complexity of the narrative is continually off-set by a certain simplicity of characterization and a certain openness of dealing with the reader: we are never deceived about who is good-hearted and who is not. In other words, Fielding has nicely calculated what kind of narrative 'good manners' are appropriate to his new literary form. For a number of fairly obvious reasons, narrative 'good manners' are of even greater importance in the drama than they are in the novel, for in the drama there are severe limitations both to the field over which a plot may operate and to an audience's powers of absorption. *Manners* were a subject to which Congreve gave a good deal of thought:

> This time, the Poet owns the bold Essay
> Yet hopes there's no ill-manners in his Play.

Thus he wrote in his prologue to *Love for Love*. It is a pity that, when writing *The Way of the World*, Congreve did not attach greater importance to another kind of 'manners', the conduct of an author towards his audience.

The play presents one other major difficulty, which is created by what might be called the Congreve glitter. This difficulty may be sensed in a variety of different ways; it turns upon the observation that Congreve's comedies possess what Dr. Johnson described as a 'wit so exuberant that it *o'er-informs its tenement*'.[1] For Dr. Johnson, as for

[1] S. Johnson, *Lives of the English Poets*, ed. G. B. Hill (Oxford, 1905), ii. 217.

Leigh Hunt after him, the difficulty seemed to lie in the 'artificial' quality of Congreve's plays. Their objection raises aesthetic problems of some complexity concerning the nature of comedy in general, and we shall have to return to these problems in due course. Other critics were more specific in their objections. It may have been Congreve whom Dryden had in mind in *A Parallel Betwixt Poetry and Painting* in 1695 when he wrote:

> I knew a poet, whom out of respect I will not name, who, being too witty himself, could draw nothing but wits in a comedy of his; even his fools were infected with the disease of their author. They overflowed with smart reparties, and were only distinguished from the intended wits by being called coxcombs, though they deserved not so scandalous a name.[1]

Pope's comment was along the same lines:

> Observe how seldom ev'n the best succeed:
> Tell me if Congreve's Fools are Fools indeed?[2]

To criticism of this kind Congreve was evidently sensitive, and it was with some acerbity that he remarked in his dedication of *The Way of the World* that hasty judges of the play seemed not to have been able 'to distinguish betwixt the Character of a *Witwoud* and a *Truewit*'. It is curious how doggedly critics have worried away at the question of whether Congreve's fools are fools indeed; to dispatch it quickly, we might say that Congreve does at least give clear warning in *The Way of the World* that we are not to think too highly of his fools : Mirabell describes Witwoud shortly before his first entrance as 'one whose Conversation can never be approv'd, yet it is now and then to be endur'd', and rebukes Petulant and Witwoud sharply enough when they threaten to walk with him in the Mall and be 'very

---

[1] *Essays of John Dryden*, ed. W. P. Ker (Oxford, 1900), ii. 141–2.
[2] 'The First Epistle of the Second Book of Horace. To Augustus', ll. 186–7.

severe' upon those they pass (I. i. 226–7, 523–8). If, despite the planting of such obvious warning-signs as these, Congreve's fools nevertheless seem to enjoy rather too generous a share of their author's quick wit, then this would seem to be only a part of a considerably larger problem concerning Congreve's power of distinguishing character through dialogue. 'Language most shows a man,' wrote Jonson; 'Speake, that I may see thee.'[1] One of Jonson's remarkable skills is that of guiding us through the complexities of his plays' plots by the means of clear individual rhythms and syntax which he gives to his different characters (a skill admirably described by Jonas Barish in his study of Jonson's prose comedies). We may often feel in listening to Congreve's verbal exchanges that, for all the rippling elegance, there is a tendency towards coalescence. According to the current view of *The Way of the World*, carefully set out by the Mueschkes and followed by later commentators such as Norman Holland, the play presents us with a central moral distinction between two ways of life: that represented by Mirabell and Mrs. Fainall, on the one hand, and that represented by Fainall and Mrs. Marwood, on the other. The vital question we must therefore ask is not whether Congreve is successful in distinguishing his Witwouds from his Truewits, but rather whether he is successful in distinguishing these two central pairs of characters. With such general difficulties and specific questions in mind we must now turn to look more closely at the play itself.

The play opens with 'Mirabell *and* Fainall *Rising from Cards*'. Mirabell has just lost the game, but offers to play on; Fainall refuses:

No, I'll give you your Revenge another time, when you are not so indifferent; you are thinking of something else now, and play

---

[1] *Discoveries*, 2031–2, in Jonson, *Works*, ed. Herford and Simpson, viii. 625.

too negligently; the Coldness of a losing Gamester lessens the Pleasure of the Winner: I'd no more play with a Man that slighted his ill Fortune, than I'd make Love to a Woman who undervalu'd the Loss of her Reputation.   (I. i. 4–10)

The gaming metaphor is used several times throughout the play to describe the particular kind of sexual struggle which is proceeding; Mirabell's reply to the speech—'You have a Taste extreamly delicate, and are for refining on your Pleasures'—is not meant to show us that Mirabell finds such an analogy distasteful, but is simply an indication that he is brooding on another matter. For Mirabell is in fact, like Fainall, a gambler in love, and it is possible to take the card-game upon which the play opens as an emblem of the action of the entire play, of the strategies that are deployed, now coolly, now passionately, on either side, for the possession of a coveted prize; though Mirabell has lost the first game, he will indeed take his 'Revenge' another time; the black box which is produced at the very end of the fifth act contains the trump card with which he will defeat Fainall and win the larger game of the play ('who's hand's out?' Petulant is to ask, entering at the critical moment: V. i. 520). Throughout the play Fainall and Mirabell will continue to converse with each other as card-players might do, saying little to each other directly, but trying to elicit information by indirect questioning and innuendo. At the moment, the precise nature of the stakes of the game between the two men is not made clear. Mirabell, if he is to win the hand of Millamant, must do so with the approval of her aunt, Lady Wishfort, or Millamant will stand to lose half of her fortune of £12,000. Later in the play, Fainall, who is now amusedly listening to Mirabell's story of how he tried to soften the aunt by an extravagant flirtation with her, will try to get his own hands on this money. But at present, it seems, it is not the money for which the two men are contending; rather, it is for Mrs. Marwood. Mrs. Marwood is Fainall's mistress; despite the secrecy of their affair, Mirabell suspects that it exists. Mrs. Marwood is also infatuated with Mirabell; Fainall suspects as much, but is seeking confirmation; he is not at all sure whether or not Mirabell has any serious interest in Mrs. Marwood. There is one further uncertainty. It is Mrs. Marwood who has informed Lady Wishfort that Mirabell's flirtation with her is simply a ruse, and who has therefore set back Mirabell's plans for winning Millamant; Mrs. Marwood's motives for doing this are not yet apparent, for it is not clear whether she has acted on Fainall's initiative or on her own. This is how Mirabell and Fainall begin to move, with cat-like wariness, to inspect such questions:

Fainall. What should provoke her to be your Enemy, without she has made you Advances, which you have slighted? Women do not easily forgive Omissions of that Nature.
Mirabell. She was always civil to me, till of late; I confess I am not one of those Coxcombs who are apt to interpret a Woman's good Manners to her Prejudice; and think that she who does not refuse 'em every thing, can refuse 'em nothing.
Fainall. You are a gallant Man, *Mirabell*; and tho' you may have Cruelty enough, not to satisfie a Lady's longing; you have too much Generosity, not to be tender of her Honour. Yet you speak with an Indifference which seems to be affected; and confesses you are conscious of a Negligence.
Mirabell. You pursue the Argument with a distrust that seems to be unaffected, and confesses you are conscious of a Concern for which the Lady is more indebted to you, than your Wife.
Fainall. Fie, fie Friend, if you grow Censorious I must leave you. . . .   (I. i. 82–100)

In this exchange the rhythms of each man's speeches are almost identical, giving a superficial impression of quickness while in fact moving slowly and guardedly; each man favours the obliqueness of double negative constructions; each man accuses the other of a failure to speak openly. Such a style, we may think, conceals its innuendoes rather too well; more damagingly, it does not allow us to glimpse any real difference between the two men. An unprepared listener might be excused for thinking at this stage that Mirabell was the greater profligate of the two, particularly as the passage follows Mirabell's flippant account of his sham courtship of the old lady.

To a large extent, of course, such false scents as these are a deliberate part of Congreve's tactics. In previous chapters we have noticed a common comic pattern which I have called comic levelling: here people of apparently different ethical beliefs, ranks and dignities, etc., are brought by the movement of the comedy to recognize their mutual kinship and equality. Comic levelling can also operate in reverse: in this case a comedy begins with two or more people who are apparently very evenly matched in strength and basically similar in their ambitions and their ethical codes, and proceeds in subsequent acts to draw out their differences, to allow victory (and some measure of approval) to one party, defeat (and some measure of disapproval) to another. The comic action here does not consist in the gradual arrival at a moral deadlock—the action of *Bartholomew Fair*, or of *The Plain Dealer*—but rather in the gradual breaking of a deadlock—the action of *The Alchemist*, and also of *The Way of the World*. Structurally speaking, the exchange between Mirabell and Fainall that we have just looked at performs the same function as the quarrel between Subtle and Face which opens *The Alchemist*: here is the deadlock; we must wait a little before we see the two men draw apart. Yet the differences between the opening scenes should also be noticed. The first is that the vulgar and direct quarrel of Jonson's play has been replaced by a gentlemanly difference of opinion, poised, brittle, characterized not by Jonsonian bluntness ('Thy worst, I fart at thee') but by excessive formality. This is quarrelling in a style to suit 'an Age more Gallant than the last'. (It is noticeable that when in the fifth act of the play Congreve imitates even more closely the actual language of the opening scene of *The Alchemist*, his imitation has an air of gentle fantastication about it, teasing out the absurdity of Lady Wishfort's wrath and humorously disguising its possible ugliness.)[1] Yet the important contrast between the two dramatists does not lie in social manners, but (again) in theatrical manners. Jonson's opening scene has no crucial expository function: it is simply a quarrel, which, by being simply a quarrel, gives unmistakable warning of the way in which the relationship between the two men is likely to develop. Further, each of Jonson's quarrellers speaks in a distinct style; and listening to their exchange, we might guess that ultimate victory could go to the cooller and more controlled of the two men.[2] The opening scene of *The Way of the World* is much more taxing to listen to, first because throughout the Mirabell–Fainall exchange Congreve scatters a number of essential items of narrative information, and secondly because of his veiled and stylistically indiscriminate prose style.

Many of the same difficulties are to be found in the scene between Mrs. Fainall and Mrs. Marwood which opens

---

[1] Thomas Davies compares the two scenes in *Dramatic Miscellanies* (London, 1784), iii. 360–1: 'they are the closest resemblances that can be found in any dramatic writings.'

[2]   *Subtle.*   No, you *scarabe*,
          I'll thunder you, in peeces. I will teach you
          How to beware, to tempt a *furie'* againe
          That carries tempest in his hand, and voice.
          Face. The place has made you valiant.   (i. i. 59–63)
The broken rhythms of Subtle's absurdly ranting blank verse ('How to beware, to tempt a *furie'* againe') already suggest a certain impotence; Face remains firm, wry, and laconic to the end (cf. his words on hearing the knocking at the door at Lovewit's return: 'Harke you, thunder' (v. iv. 137)).

the second act. Once again the individual voices of the speakers are not clearly distinguished, and once again the mutual accusations of affectation and insincerity make it difficult for us to know what is to be believed and what is to be rejected. The act opens with longish, swaying, sententious speeches from each of the two women, rhythmically and tonally very near to one another; then moves to this terse and edgy exchange:

Mrs. Marwood. And yet I am thinking sometimes, to carry my Aversion further.

Mrs. Fainall. How?

Mrs. Marwood. Faith by Marrying; if I cou'd but find one that lov'd me very well, and would be thoroughly sensible of ill usage; I think I shou'd do my self the violence of undergoing the Ceremony.

Mrs. Fainall. You would not make him a Cuckold?

Mrs. Marwood. No; but I'd make him believe I did, and that's as bad.

Mrs. Fainall. Why, had not you as good do it?

Mrs. Marwood. O if he shou'd ever discover it, he wou'd then know the worst; and be out of his Pain; but I wou'd have him ever continue upon the Rack of Fear and Jealousy.

Mrs. Fainall. Ingenious mischief! Wou'd thou wert married to *Mirabell.*

Mrs. Marwood. Wou'd I were.

Mrs. Fainall. You change Colour.

Mrs. Marwood. Because I hate him.

Mrs. Fainall. So do I; but I can hear him nam'd.

(II. i. 50–70)

Dr. Johnson's description of Congreve's characters as 'intellectual gladiators'—'every sentence is to ward or strike'[1]—seems very exact here. At first glance, this darting exchange might seem to anticipate the best scenes of reported dialogue in Richardson's *Clarissa*; yet if on

[1] Op. cit. ii. 228.

reflection the dialogue seems altogether less good than Richardson's (or, closer to home, than Etherege's: one might compare the scene in the third act of *The Man of Mode* where Bellinda professes a dislike of Dorimant in order to hear what Emilia and Lady Townley really think of him), it may be because of the constant presence in the passage of a mild humorous inflation. Mrs. Marwood's and Mrs. Fainall's struggle to contain a deep mutual hostility by means of a formal politeness never becomes openly comic, in the manner of, say, the encounter of Polly and Lucy in the third act of *The Beggar's Opera*, or of Gwendolen and Cecily in the second act of *The Importance of Being Earnest*; yet there is a constant undercurrent of absurdity. Marwood's threatened revenge on the male sex is quite as ludicrous as Lady Wishfort's threatened revenge on Mirabell later in the play: 'I'll have him poyson'd. Where does he eat? *I'll marry a Drawer* to have him poyson'd in his Wine' (III. i. 102–4). The dialogue shimmers uneasily between high passion and high comedy, without decisively registering either mood; it is rather too careful and too comic to convey the quick, spontaneous nervous energies of a real-life exchange.

The early part of the play, then, for all its subtle brilliance, sets up a number of frustrations, concerning plot, characters, and tone; some of these frustrations, though they may seem ill-judged, seem also to have been brought in quite deliberately as a kind of intellectual stimulus. As the second act proceeds, Congreve begins to sketch in more firmly the individual outlines of his characters and to allow their distinctive voices to be heard; the situation is now more rapidly displayed. As in a formal dance, the couples in St. James's Park now begin to pair, then part, then pair again in different combinations. Three couples are displayed in successive scenes. First come a pair of adulterers, Fainall and Marwood; their exchanges are heavy, passionate, mutually recriminatory. Next come a pair who have lived together outside wedlock, though they are not technically adulterers, Mirabell and Mrs. Fainall; there is still some passion and recrimination here, but they argue more steadily and reasonably together. Last come the pair who will eventually go into marriage, Mirabell and Millamant; here there is neither heavy passion nor everyday reasonableness; their affection expresses itself in wit. The first pair are sententious: 'But cou'd you think because the nodding Husband would not wake, that e'er the watchful Lover slept!'; the last pair, thanks to Millamant's energies ('Sententious *Mirabell*!'), are never allowed to be. The first pair are in all senses of the word solitary; the last pair meet in company, and are separated from each other by the absurd figure of Witwoud. His presence between them— 'like a Skreen before a great Fire'—nicely restrains the possible romanticism of the meeting, in much the same fashion that the presence of the fat Mrs. Musgrove, formidably placed between Anne Elliot and Captain Wentworth as they sit together on the same sofa in their first meeting after many years' separation, acts as a comic control to sentiment in Chapter 8 of Jane Austen's *Persuasion*—'It was no inconsiderable barrier, indeed.' With the arrival of Millamant a new and quite distinctive gaiety enters the play. She is described as a whirlwind and as a windmill, she declares that 'one makes Lovers as fast as one pleases', her very name suggests that she has a thousand loves; yet like Rosalind in *As You Like It* threatening to be 'more giddy in my desires than a monkey', Millamant is the rock upon whose steadiness the entire action of the play depends; of the three pairs of lovers the act has shown us, Millamant is the only individual who is both chaste and constant. The second act is thus built upon a careful structure of comparisons and constrasts between the three pairs of lovers and ex-lovers; its architecture deserves admiration. But there is one curiously vulnerable point in the structure, which affects the way in which we take the whole play: this is to be found in the encounter between Mirabell and Mrs. Fainall.

Mrs. Fainall is a remarkable variant upon a stock type of Restoration comedy, the cast mistress. Unlike the usual representative of this type (Mrs. Loveit in *The Man of Mode*, for instance), Mrs. Fainall remains affectionate and kindly disposed towards Mirabell, and is unselfish enough to help him towards marriage with Millamant. It is important for the moral balance of the play that we sense some reciprocal affection on Mirabell's part towards Mrs. Fainall, but not so much as would make his present courtship of Millamant seem disturbing. It is a delicate matter. How has Mirabell treated Mrs. Fainall in the past? And what is his present relationship with her? The following exchange is evidently designed to clarify these questions:

> *Mrs. Fainall.* . . . Why did you make me marry this Man?
> *Mirabell.* Why do we daily commit disagreeable and dangerous Actions? To save that Idol Reputation. If the familiarities of our Loves had produc'd that Consequence, of which you were apprehensive, where could you have fix'd a Father's Name with Credit, but on a Husband? I knew *Fainall* to be a Man lavish of his Morals, an interested and professing Friend, a false and designing Lover; yet one whose Wit and outward fair behaviour have gain'd a Reputation with the Town, enough to make that Woman stand excus'd, who has suffer'd herself to be won by his Addresses. A better man ought not to have been sacrific'd to the Occasion; a worse had not answer'd to the Purpose. When you are weary of him, you know your Remedy.   (II. i. 263–77)

Presumably the speech is meant to let us know that the affair between Mirabell and Mrs. Fainall is now honourably at an end; and also that Fainall, however smooth appearances may be, is not a man to be trusted (and in this last respect the speech fulfils a function somewhat like Mirabell's earlier speech which warns us about Witwoud: 'He is one whose Conversation can never be approv'd . . .' etc.). The speech's crucial function, then, is to distinguish clearly for the first time between Mirabell's way of life and Fainall's. On every point the speech clumsily misfires (except, arguably, in its denigration of Fainall; indeed, it is difficult to know how that speech could be entirely successful *both* at denigrating Fainall and at exculpating Mirabell). Mrs. Fainall's plain question seems to demand a plain answer. Mirabell's reply is elegant but devious; it has an unfortunate briskness about it, a half-jocularity, an air of tossing the question somewhat lightly aside. One reason for the apparent evasiveness is that Congreve was still smarting from Collier's attack on the indecencies of contemporary comedy; judged by the standards of its day (and of our own: compare this discussion with that of Honey's hysterical pregnancy in *Who's Afraid of Virginia Woolf*) *The Way of the World* is particularly reticent in its treatment of the physical aspects of sexual relationships; later the fact of Fainall's and Marwood's adultery is conveyed to Lady Wishfort in a whisper which the audience is not allowed to hear (v. i. 472–3). Yet this 'politeness' can also look like superficiality and callousness on Mirabell's part: he admits that he knows Fainall to be a thoroughly perfidious man, yet he has had no hesitation in marrying off his mistress to Fainall to get himself out of a sticky situation. A concern for 'Reputation' is offered as the mainspring of Mirabell's action, yet it is hard not to feel that a more pressing reason is Congreve's need to allow Mirabell to prosecute his affair with Millamant. And why, we may ask, should Mirabell, who has been so severe about the shortcomings of poor

Witwoud's 'wit', tolerate as a suitable husband for his ex-mistress 'one whose Wit and outward fair Behaviour have gain'd a Reputation with the Town, enough to make that Woman stand excus'd, who has suffer'd herself to be won by his Addresses'. Isn't Fainall's kind of 'wit' more intolerable than Witwoud's? At this point Congreve's style begins to crack up more seriously. To say to one's mistress that 'A better man ought not to have been *sacrific'd* to the Occasion' must sound particularly offensive; Congreve is not wanting to make Mirabell sound offensive, but is merely continuing in a decidedly maladroit way a metaphor which he opened at the beginning of the speech, about 'that Idol Reputation'. The last sentence of Mirabell's speech carries even more seriously misleading suggestions: 'When you are weary of him, you know your Remedy.' Mrs. Fainall's 'remedy' is in fact the deed of conveyance which she has entrusted to Mirabell, which will ensure her financial independence. We do not know this until right at the very end of the play, by which time this particular line will almost certainly have been forgotten, and the subtlety of the reference lost. The obvious and immediate way to take the line is to assume that Mirabell means that Mrs. Fainall may return to be his mistress any time she pleases. Evidently the affair between Mirabell and Mrs. Fainall is in fact meant to be decisively at an end; if it is not, then a cloud of moral doubt hangs over Mirabell's pursuit of Millamant, and we shall see him not as a reformed philanderer but as an active one, who, like Etherege's Dorimant, keeps several irons in the fire at once. In this case the clear moral distinction which critics claim to find between the characters of Mirabell and Fainall becomes a little hard to see. Throughout the play there are several suggestions that the Mirabell–Mrs. Fainall affair is still alive. Shortly before the speech we have just looked at, Mirabell has said to Mrs. Fainall, 'You shou'd have just so much disgust for your Husband, as may be sufficient to make you relish your Lover' (II. i. 258–60). In the following act Mrs. Fainall does not contradict Foible when the maid declares that it must be more than a matter of a 'former good Correspondence' between Mrs. Fainall and Mirabell: 'Sweet Lady, to be so good! Mr. *Mirabell* cannot chuse but be grateful. I find your Ladyship has his Heart still' (III. i. 197, 203–5). These hints seem to be deliberately laid as part of another narrative false scent; the purpose is evidently to thicken the apparent complications in the way of an ultimate match between Mirabell and Millament, and to heighten our pleasure in Act IV, when we find that we have overestimated these complications, and that Mrs. Fainall is not a rival for Mirabell's love but rather a disinterested helper. Yet such narrative subtlety is dearly bought; the price is clarity of moral design.

The third act of the play may be more rapidly passed over. It introduces two new characters, Lady Wishfort and Sir Wilfull Witwoud, and a counterplot: Marwood and Fainall learn of Mirabell's affair with Mrs. Fainall and of his plot to have his servant Waitwell woo Lady Wishfort in the person of 'Sir Rowland', and resolve to gain control of the whole of Mrs. Fainall's fortune and of one-half of Mrs. Millamant's. The remarkable fourth act, however, deserves rather closer examination. The counterplotters, Fainall and Mrs. Marwood, disappear entirely from this act (as Mirabell has disappeared from the third act); as a result, the busy part of the plot comes to a virtual standstill, and Congreve has an opportunity to develop the poised and leisurely style at which he most excels. The mood of the act is genial, expansive, a little heady; four proposals are made, a bottle or two is uncorked, a few songs are sung, some poetry absently recited; there is a dance; the action sprawls agreeably before the final rapid collection of narrative threads in the catastrophe of the piece. The succession of proposal scenes presents a series of contrasts in the same manner as the succession of lovers' meetings in the second act. The variations in courting style are expertly played over: the proposals are, in turn, gauche (Sir Wilfull), poised (Mirabell), blunt (Petulant), and sham (Waitwell). The last proposal in this sequence is heralded first; Lady Wishfort's meticulous preparation for Sir Rowland's arrival sets the leisured tempo of the act:

Lady Wishfort. Well, and how shall I receive him? In what figure shall I give his Heart the first Impression? There is a great deal in the first Impression. Shall I sit?—No I won't sit—I'll walk—aye I'll walk from the door upon his entrance; and then turn full upon him—No, that will be too sudden. I'll lie—aye, I'll lie down—I'll receive him in my little dressing Room, there's a Couch—Yes, yes, I'll give the first Impression on a Couch—I won't lie neither but loll and lean upon one Elbow; with one Foot a little dangling off, Jogging in a thoughtful way—Yes—and then as soon as he appears, start, ay, start and be surpriz'd, and rise to meet him in a pretty disorder—Yes—O, nothing is more alluring than a Levee from a Couch in some Confusion.—It shows the Foot to advantage, and furnishes with Blushes, and re-composing Airs beyond Comparison. Hark! There's a Coach. (IV. i. 17–32)

Airs is a favourite word of Millamant's; her first words have been 'O I have deny'd my self Airs to Day' (II. i. 333–4); later Mrs. Marwood rebukes her, 'Indeed, my Dear, you'll tear another Fan, if you don't mitigate those violent Airs' (III. i. 333–4). The word ranges in sense from 'liberty' (the freedom of walking in the open air, is what Millamant's phrase means) to 'affected tantrums' (Marwood's sense) and 'feminine graces' (Lady Wishfort's sense); the word provides an important emotional key to the act. The fact that both Lady Wishfort and Millamant use the word effects a

brief comic identification of the two; an identification that
is strengthened by the fact that Millamant is now preparing
for her own suitor with the same studied negligence as her
aunt. It is Sir Wilfull Witwoud she is apparently preparing
to meet; her aunt has insisted that she hear his suit. But
she knows that Mirabell is in the house and that he wants
to see her; as in Act II it is a Witwoud who temporarily
keeps the lovers apart.

It has been suggested (by Kenneth Muir) that Millamant's
quotations from Suckling and Waller during this scene
indicate her intelligent awareness of the real issues at stake
as she stands at the verge of matrimony; for the poems from
which the lines are taken deal with the theme of inconstancy
in love.[1] But the point of the quotations is not that they
indicate any real depth of moral reflection in Millamant
(the sentiments expressed in the poems are no more than
wispy commonplaces) but rather that they establish something about her style and taste: 'Well, an illiterate Man's
my Aversion', she has declared to Petulant and Witwoud
earlier in the play, 'I wonder at the impudence of any
Illiterate Man, to offer to make Love' (III. i. 422–4). The
point is a comic one, and the joke is half on Millamant:

Millamant (Repeating).
        I swear it will not do its part,
        Tho' thou do'st thine, employ'st the Power and Art.
Natural, easie *Suckling*!
Sir Wilfull. Anan? *Suckling*? No such Suckling neither, Cozen,
nor Stripling: I thank Heav'n, I'm no Minor.
Millamant. Ah Rustick! ruder than *Gothick*.
Sir Wilfull. Well, well, I shall understand your *Lingo* one of these
days, Cozen, in the mean while, I must answer in plain *English*.
                                                                (IV. i. 104–12)

---

[1] Kenneth Muir, 'The Comedies of William Congreve', in *Restoration
Theatre*, eds. J. R. Brown and Bernard Harris, Stratford-upon-Avon Studies 6
(London, 1965), pp. 232–4.

Millamant herself will soon have to abandon her 'lingo' and declare her love for Mirabell in the way Mrs. Fainall bids her, 'in plain terms' (IV. i. 292), moving from the exquisite artificialities of Suckling into the real world of marriage. The comedy highlights not simply the shortcomings of Sir Wilfull's stubborn illiteracy but also the shortcomings of Millamant's equally stubborn literacy, as she attempts to take refuge from life in art. It is comedy of mutual discomfiture and mutual incomprehension; Fielding caught its style faithfully enough in *Tom Jones* when he allowed Mrs. Western, in debate with her brother, to allude with a similar loftiness to her reading in philosophy:

'Have I not told you what Plato says on that subject—a subject on which you was so notoriously ignorant when you first came under my care, that I verily believe you did not know the relation between a daughter and a father'.—''Tis a lie', answered Western. 'The girl is no such fool, as to live to eleven years old without knowing that she was her father's relation'.—'O! more than Gothic ignorance', answered the lady. 'And as for your manners, brother, I must tell you, they deserve a cane . . . It is impossible, it is impossible', cries the aunt; 'no one can undervalue such a boor'.—'Boar', answered the squire, 'I am no boar; no, nor ass; no, nor rat neither madam. Remember that—I am no rat.' (VIII. iii)

Millamant's quotations also have a literary ancestry. 'Natural, easie *Suckling*!' is probably a memory of Rochester ('Suckling's easie Pen'); she quotes Waller after the same fashion that Dorimant quotes Waller throughout *The Man of Mode*, and one remembers that John Dennis declared that Dorimant's quotations from Waller were one of several characteristics that revealed that the character was modelled on Rochester himself.[1] Mirabell enters to complete a couplet

[1] 'Satyr ⟨Commonly called Timon, a Satyr⟩', 105, in *Poems by John Wilmot Earl of Rochester*, ed. Vivian de Sola Pinto (London, 1953), p. 102; *The Critical Works of John Dennis*, ed. E. N. Hooker (Baltimore, 1943), ii. 248.

from Waller which Millamant has begun, just as Harriet in *The Man of Mode* completes the Waller couplet which Dorimant has on his lips as he comes in; in each case, literary compatibility, at least, seems to be assured:

> *Enter* Dorimant.
> *Dorimant. Musick so softens and disarms the mind.*
> *Harriet. That not one Arrow does resistance find.*
> (*The Man of Mode*, v. ii. 92–3)
>
> *Millamant. . . . Like* Phoebus *sung the no less am'rous Boy.*
> *Enter* Mirabell.
> *Mirabell. Like* Daphne *she as lovely and as Coy.*
> (*The Way of the World*, iv. i. 153–5)

The celebrated 'proviso' scene likewise has a literary ancestry, as Kathleen Lynch has shown; in this case the ancestry is longer and more complex, and Congreve plays brilliant variations upon the familiar themes.[1] One example (it is one of the very few analogues to have escaped Miss Lynch's eagle eye) will be enough to show Congreve's method and his superiority. At the end of Wycherley's *The Gentleman Dancing-Master* Mrs. Flirt, a 'Common woman of the town', strikes up a bargain with Monsieur de Paris to settle the details of their living together—'according to the honourable Institution of Keeping, come'. The talk turns at once to questions of maintenance money, town houses and their furniture, coaches and horses, servants, clothes, jewellery—and to the question of the mistress's privacy:

Monsieur. Well, is this all?

Flirt. No then, that when you come to my house, you never presume to touch a key, lift up a Latch, or thrust a Door, without knocking before hand; and that you ask no questions, if you see a stray piece of Plate, Cabinet, or Looking-glass in my house.

Monsieur. Just a Wife in every thing; but what else?   (v. i.)

[1] Kathleen M. Lynch, 'D'Urfé's *L'Astrée* and the Proviso Scenes in Dryden's Comedy', *P.Q.* iv (October 1925), pp. 302–8.

Millamant and Mirabell's talk, on the other hand, scarcely touches upon such cold mercantile facts as these (there will be a time to settle these, in the following act); their luxurious concentration upon the minutiae of domestic life implicitly suggests that upon fundamentals they are already agreed. Millamant's insistence that her privacy be respected—'And lastly, where ever I am, you shall always knock at the door before you come in' (IV. i. 223–5)—is to preserve her 'dear Liberty' within marriage, but it is not, like Mrs. Flirt's similar insistence, to preserve a liberty to prosecute other intrigues.[1] (And the claim has a certain situational humour, for Mirabell has just cornered Millamant in a locked room, having entered without knocking to elicit these very terms.) Above all, Congreve perfectly controls the tone of the dialogue; Mirabell's coolness—'Have you any more Conditions to offer? Hitherto your demands are pretty reasonable' (IV. i. 210–11)—manages to suggest an undercurrent of affection in a way that Monsieur's coolness—'Just a Wife in every thing; but what else?'—simply does not; one might contrast Congreve's less happy depiction of Mirabell's coolness in his scene with Mrs. Fainall in the second act.

The entry, one after another, of Witwoud, Petulant, and

---

[1] There is a similar change of emphasis in the way Congreve adapts a passage from Jonson's *The Devil is an Ass* in this scene. In II. i. 160–7 Fitzdottrell instructs Pug to keep a watch on his wife's possible intrigues:

> Be you sure, now,
> Yo' haue all your eyes about you; and let in
> No lace-woman; nor bawd, that brings French-masques,
> And cut-works. See you? Nor old croans, with wafers,
> To conuey letters. Nor no youths, disguis'd
> Like country-wiues, with creame, and marrow-puddings.
> Much knauery may be vented in a pudding,
> Much bawdy intelligence: They'are shrewd ciphers.

Mirabell forbids Millamant her traffic with 'all Bauds with Baskets', etc. (IV. i. 247–54), not because he fears smuggled love-letters but because he fears smuggled medicinal and cosmetic preparations. Congreve's lovers stand above jealousy.

Sir Wilfull in different stages of intoxication provides a broad outlet for the accumulated high spirits which have been building up throughout this act. The effect is like that which Fielding creates at the end of *Tom Jones* with the last whirlwind entry of Squire Western just as Sophia and Tom move in slow and delicate steps towards matrimony:

At this instant Western, who had stood some time listening, burst into the room, and, with his hunting voice and phrase, cried out, 'To her, boy, go to her.—That's it, little honeys, O that's it! Well, what, is it all over? Hath she appointed the day, boy? What, shall it be tomorrow or next day? It shan't be put off a minute longer than next day, I am resolved'.   (xviii. xii)

Unlike Squire Western, Petulant and the Witwouds are too self-immersed to encourage the couple's mutual affection in quite this way; Petulant, off-handed and drunk, throws yet another proposal in Millamant's way: 'Look you, Mrs. *Millamant*,—If you can love me dear Nymph—say it—and that's the Conclusion—pass on, or pass off,—that's all' (IV. i. 339–41). In a comedy which has made so many of its effects through hint, nuance, and euphemism the introduction of bluntness and a certain rugged joviality at this stage provides a sudden sense of release: '*In vino veritas*', declares Sir Wilfull, who has been celebrating the accomplishment of his kind of liberty while Millamant has been ensuring the accomplishment of her kind. Sir Wilfull's song—'We'll drink and we'll never ha' done Boys'—brings him to express a traditional figure of inverted order with which we are by now thoroughly familiar: 'The Sun's a good Pimple, an honest Soaker, he has a Cellar at your *Antipodes*. If I travel Aunt, I touch at your *Antipodes*—your *Antipodes* are a good rascally sort of topsy-turvey Fellows —If I had a Bumper I'd stand upon my Head and drink a Health to 'em . . .' (IV. i. 422–6). The image of the inverted antipodeans tipsily saluted by an inverted Sir Wilfull analogically conveys the happy eruptions of the main plot, where Millamant and Mirabell resolve to go into marriage contrary to the express wishes of Lady Wishfort, turning upside-down the world of authority which she still, in her frail way, represents. We are not allowed to forget that their coming-together, for all its obvious emotional rightness, is nevertheless an act of disobedience; nor are we allowed to forget that the machinery of the outside plots has still been left whirring. The fourth act celebrates not only the achievement of human sociability— giving us the union of the gay couple, the blessing upon their marriage of the apparent rival, Mrs. Fainall, the amicability of the Witwoud half-brothers (and hence, by extension, a *rapprochement* of town and country), Petulant's kiss of Sir Wilfull 'in a humour of reconciliation'— it celebrates too, in a variety of complex ways, the achievement of 'liberty' and freedom from restraint. Union and independence, agreement and disobedience, concord and discord are held in delicate balance throughout the act, a balance that might be described in Jack Cade's words, 'then are we in order when we are most out of order' (*2 Henry VI*, iv. iii. 199).

The Way of the World does not end there, as it might have done, upon the happiness which follows the girl's granting of her consent; events must first return more decisively to order, and liberty must be more precisely defined. In an earlier chapter we noticed that one of the problems that the comic dramatist faces is that of negotiating the transition from the world of festivity and possible lawlessness which the comedy brings into being, re-entering the world of everyday law and order, and reconciling the feeling of exuberant comic release with a recognition of the cold problems of day-to-day experience. Congreve allows the whole of the fifth act to manage this re-entry.

In the fifth act the notion of liberty is complemented by another notion: that of legality; taken together, these two themes resemble the theme of 'licence' which Jonson explored in *Bartholomew Fair*. As the act proceeds, so too does the flurrying accumulation of legal documents; the action is knotted with red tape, first this way, then that. At the end of the fourth act, an anonymous letter (in fact from Marwood) has told Lady Wishfort that the 'Sir Rowland' who is now courting her is a fraud. Undeterred, Waitwell promises to fetch verification: 'But some proof you must let me give you;—I'll go for a black box, which Contains the Writings of my whole Estate, and deliver that into your hands' (IV. i. 632–5). Waitwell's box is to play a crucial part in bringing about what Congreve called 'the artful Solution of the *Fable*'; as a comic device, it has a distant ancestor in the casket of Plautus' *Cistellaria* and a distant descendant in the famous handbag which resolves the action of *The Importance of Being Earnest*. Yet, as I have suggested in Chapter Three, it has an even closer relative in the black box of Jonson's *Bartholomew Fair*, which contains Cokes's wedding licence; like this box, Waitwell's takes on an almost symbolic importance; it is to be a physical reminder of the law's power as a 'solution', a way to liberty. But just now, in a dense and rapid sequence of events, the law is being used to bind: between the acts, as Waitwell has gone to fetch the box, Fainall has had him arrested; Marwood meanwhile has assured Lady Wishfort more openly that 'Sir Rowland' is a fraud; and she has revealed at the same time that Mirabell and Mrs. Fainall have been lovers. Fainall's brazen claim is that Mrs. Fainall (because of her past liaison with Mirabell) and Millamant (because of her intended future liaison with Mirabell, contrary to her aunt's wishes) both stand in disgrace; and that the remainder of Mrs. Fainall's fortune and the half of Millamant's must consequently be made over to himself. But why, Lady Wishfort very reasonably suggests, should not the law be used to provide a release from this disgrace; if Fainall feels so strongly, why should he not divorce his wife? This is not the way Fainall will have the law work for him; and he insists that he will prepare for Lady Wishfort's signature two 'instruments' which will ensure the transfer of the two fortunes. More paper. Meanwhile we learn that the informal swapping of terms between Millamant and Mirabell has led to a formal contract of marriage, which is now being drawn up. Another marriage contract is also in preparation: for Waitwell has asked Lady Wishfort if, while he fetches his black box, he may also 'presume to bring a Contract to be sign'd this Night?' (iv. i. 638–9), and has received a happy answer. Millamant, now seemingly penitent, announces that she has no intention of displeasing her aunt, and that she will resign her marriage contract to her at once. Another contract: Mirabell and Sir Wilfull have contracted in an informal way to travel together, on 'proviso' that Sir Wilfull will first marry Millamant; the whole bargain, Sir Wilfull generously protests, is hardly binding ('My contract went no further than a little Mouth-Glew, and that's hardly dry': v. i. 396–7). Lady Wishfort agrees that she will forgive Mirabell, but 'on *proviso*' that he immediately resigns his contract to marry Millamant (v. i. 403). Mirabell at once agrees: 'It is in Writing and with Papers of Concern; but I have sent my Servant for it, and will deliver it to you, with all acknowledgements for your transcendent goodness' (v. i. 405–7). Mirabell's servant is of course Waitwell; Waitwell is Sir Rowland; Sir Rowland has already gone for a variety of papers of his own. '*Enter* Waitwell *with a Box of Writings.*' 'I have brought the Black box at last, *Madam*' (v. i. 508, 510–11). The complexity of this stage of the play is of quite a different order from the occasionally vexatious complexity of the earlier acts. What the fifth act spectacularly displays is a theme which has been glimpsed frequently throughout the play as a whole: namely, the variety of ways in which duties and relationships may be enforced and avoided. Kinship provides one kind of bond, so too does the sexual relationship. A promise is another kind of bond: a promise to marry, like Millamant's to Mirabell, or to travel, like Mirabell's to Sir Wilfull, or to keep a secret, like the promise which Mincing and Foible found themselves forced to take when they came upon Fainall and Mrs. Marwood together in the blue garret. Yet such bonds as these can also be broken: it is possible to disown a half-brother and to get rid of a mistress, to forgo an agreement to marry if the marriage does not meet with the approval of one's guardian, it is possible to call off a pact to be 'sworn Brothers and fellow Travellers' (v. i. 346–7) if one's sworn brother is in obvious distress; it is even possible, as Fainall and Marwood find to their cost, to break an oath of secrecy if it is only made 'upon *Messalina*'s Poems', and a 'Bible-oath' is taken in its place (v. i. 488, 478). Even physical force—Sir Wilfull's flourishing of his 'Instrument' (a sword) against Fainall's (a legal deed: v. i. 428–9)—may be ineffectual, as Norman Holland points out in a perceptive discussion of this aspect of the play.[1] Only the law has final power to bind or to release; yet the law must be sound law. Fainall's law is mere bluff, for he has no power to enforce the threats he makes to Lady Wishfort; further, his law is imperfectly negotiated, for the deed which he has made to seize part of his wife's fortune turns out to be invalid. Mirabell is victorious at the end of the play not because of any particular moral qualities he may have, but rather because he is

[1] Op. cit., p. 181. Both Norman Holland's and the Mueschkes' accounts of the fifth act of the play are particularly helpful.

a better lawyer than Fainall, and has made sure that his threats and his bargains are legally enforceable. He has taken the precaution of marrying Waitwell to Foible before putting the 'Sir Rowland' plot into action:

> *Mrs. Fainall.* So, if my poor Mother is caught in a Contract, you will discover the Imposture betimes; and release her by producing a Certificate of her Gallants former Marriage.
> *Mirabell.* Yes, upon Condition she consent to my Marriage with her Niece, and surrender the Moiety of her Fortune in her Possession. (II. i. 296–303)

The explanation of this plan in the second act of the play, combined with Waitwell's request to Lady Wishfort at the end of the fourth act that he may be allowed to return to her with a marriage contract, sets up an expectation that the 'Certificate of her Gallants former Marriage' will be the crucial document which effects the play's denouement; and this certificate (one may be allowed to think) must be among those other 'Writings of my whole Estate', those 'Papers of Concern' of which both Waitwell and Mirabell have spoken (IV. i. 634, V. i. 405). The document which Mirabell in fact pulls out of the black box is a deed of conveyance of the whole estate of Mrs. Fainall on trust to Mirabell, negotiated before her marriage to Fainall, duly signed by two witnesses, Petulant and Witwoud, according to 'the Laws of this Land'.

In *The Plain Dealer* we noticed that Manly's victory over Olivia is achieved outside 'the Laws of this Land', and that in strict legal terms Olivia would seem to have right on her side. Much of the satirical energy of *The Plain Dealer* is, of course, directed against the conventional ways of the world, and most notably against its laws and its lawyers; the 're-entry' of the comedy into this actual world is finally made, as we have seen, with wariness and a little ambiguity. *The Way of the World*, on the other hand, moves firmly to an endorsement of the forms and conventions of civilized society: it celebrates not only the virtues of delicious irresponsibility—lying abed in a morning as long as one pleases, pinning up one's hair with verse—but also the virtues of harnessing some of the energies of wit to the management of everyday affairs. So far from closing on a romantic upbeat, at the happy prospect of marriage, the play looks in a practical way at the possible outcome of marriages that are not entered into with care and love: at the possible facts of adultery, of widowhood, and of divorce. The play's values are, in all senses of that word, those of *urbanity*; its 'world' is the world of civilized town society; the amiable presence of Sir Wilfull Witwoud with his improbable plans for travel, and the wider geographical references of the play (to the Russian czar, the antipodeans, the Tartars and Turks and Saracens), serve finally only to highlight the attractiveness of this smaller world, the London *beau monde*.

Congreve is perhaps the last major English writer to celebrate this kind of worldliness in this kind of way. 'The little world' was how Fielding, a West Country man, was to describe the town society which formed Congreve's main subject (*Tom Jones*, xv. iii). To Clarissa Harlowe in London, Anna Howe was to write apprehensively, 'You are in the *world* now, you know' (Everyman edn., vol. ii, Letter LVII), and it was with a similar apprehensiveness that Fanny Burney would describe another 'Young Lady's entrance to the World'. To an eighteenth-century eye this world could seem not only geographically confined but even a little sinister. Occasionally the point is actually conveyed by precise echoes of Congreve's play: consider the way in which George Lillo in *The London Merchant* allows the scheming Millwood to speak with the very accents of Lady Wishfort as she lies in wait for the man she intends to ruin—'Now, after what manner shall I receive him?' (I. iv. 4)[1]—or the way in which Fielding imitates parts of *The Way of the World*, including the proviso scene, in *The Modern Husband* (1732), in order to place at a critical distance the manners and morals of Congreve's age. 'Vanbrugh and Congreve copied nature,' Fielding wrote in *Tom Jones* (xiv. i), 'but they who copy them draw as unlike the present age as Hogarth would do if he was to paint a rout, or a drum, in the dresses of Titian and of Vandyke.' Though Congreve portrayed his age accurately enough, the times have now changed; Dryden had said the same of Jonson in his epilogue to the second part of *The Conquest of Granada*; in each case there is a feeling that the writers of 'the last age' may have possessed a greater genius than those of the present age, but that they also tolerated the manners of their day in a way which would no longer be entirely acceptable. Dryden disliked the coarseness of Jonson's plays, which he thought was a reflection of the coarseness of Jonson's age; for Fielding what was suspect was the *politeness* of Congreve and his age. 'What the world generally calls politeness', declared Fielding's Amelia, 'I term insincerity.'[2] Fielding contrasts the 'sincerity' and 'tenderness' of Amelia and Booth with the 'very polite' relationship of Colonel James and his wife, who maintain—as Mirabell and Millamant have pretended they will—a cool independence within marriage, never seeing one another each day until dinner-time. Richard Steele, who, like Fielding, was a warm admirer of Congreve, could also eye *Millamantism* with equal mistrust: 'a woman's man should conceal passion

---

[1] William H. McBurney points out the echo in his edition of *The London Merchant* (London, 1965), Introduction, p. xix. In Charles Johnson's *Caelia: or, the Perjur'd Lover* (1733) the villainous Wronglove (a prototype for Richardson's Lovelace) sends his unsuspecting mistress to a brothel with a quotation from Congreve on his lips.

[2] *Amelia*, v. iii. The 'very polite scene' between the Jameses takes place in xi. i. Amelia expresses a gently ironical opinion upon Congreve's 'Love's but a frailty of the mind' in vi. iii.

in a familiar air of indifference', declared Steele's Mrs. Clerimont in *The Tender Husband* (v. i.), 'Now there's Mr. Clerimont; I can't allow him the least freedom, but the unfashionable fool grows so fond of me he cannot hide it in public.' But in the comedy of the early eighteenth century such an 'unfashionable fool' as Mr. Clerimont was no longer to be laughed at; it was the mocker who was mocked.

New moral sensitivities bring into being new kinds of comedy. Because so much of the new eighteenth-century comedy is inferior, we tend to underrate the importance of the shift in feeling which brought it about; but it is a shift whose first, major tremors Congreve felt strongly enough as he wrote, and which has permanently affected the way in which we think and talk about comedy today. Although the criticism of Congreve's plays in the eighteenth century could often be naïve, it could also—like Collier himself—sometimes be acute. Take, for instance, this discussion of *Love for Love* which takes place in Fanny Burney's *Evelina* (Letter xx) after a performance of the play at Drury Lane:

'Angelica', cried Sir Clement, 'is a noble girl; she tries her lover severely, but she rewards him generously.' 'Yet in a trial so long', said Mrs. Mirvan, 'there seems rather too much consciousness of her power.'

'Since my opinion has the sanction of Mrs. Mirvan's', added Lord Orville, 'I will venture to say, that Angelica bestows her hand rather with the air of a benefactress, than with the tenderness of a mistress. Generosity without delicacy, like wit without judgement, generally gives as much pain as pleasure. The uncertainty in which she keeps Valentine, and her manner of trifling with his temper, give no very favourable idea of her own.'

What is particularly telling about this exact and fastidious criticism of the play is that it recalls, and yet quite surpasses, the *apparent* exactitude and fastidiousness of Congreve's own prose ('For a passionate Lover, methinks you are a Man somewhat discerning in the Failings of your Mistress', etc.), probing questions of behaviour with a Johnsonian seriousness where Congreve moves formally across them with a sweeping glissade. Congreve's plays may expose the failings of 'wit without judgement'; Lord Orville's criticism is a reminder that there may be other, equally important failings ('generosity without delicacy') which his plays appear to ignore. There is no good reason why a comedy should be considered to fall short of full success because it does not achieve a moral definition as delicate as that of Fanny Burney or of Dr. Johnson; freighted with such eighteenth-century judgement as theirs, a comedy might indeed well disappear for ever beneath the waves. And yet one may continue to feel that there are areas of Congreve's comedies which are morally bothering: Valentine's jocular callousness towards his former mistress in *Love for Love*, for instance, and his light suggestion that the child she has had by him might as well be suffocated; the decidedly cruel jokes which Mirabell plays upon Lady Wishfort as he elbows his way towards his wife and his fortune; the fact that while he prudently looks after Mrs. Fainall's finances, Mirabell does not apparently care what happens to her happiness (the play leads us to ask what life for her with Fainall will be like after Mirabell has played his last stunning trick, and secured his own happiness).[1] We bother about such points because Congreve continually

---

[1] Cf. John Wain, 'Restoration Comedy and its Modern Critics', in *Preliminary Essays* (London, 1957), pp. 1–35; G. Wilson Knight, *The Golden Labyrinth* (London, 1962), p. 135 (a brief but particularly telling sketch of the play's weaknesses). Richardson's Lovelace looks after his women in rather the same style as Mirabell, taking care 'to marry off a former mistress, if possible, before I took to a new one' (*Clarissa*, ii, Letter XLI). Jean Gagen provides a singularly unconvincing defence of Mirabell's conduct in 'Congreve's Mirabell and the Ideal of the Gentleman', *P.M.L.A.* (September 1964), pp. 422–7.

invites us to bother about other points of equal nicety concerning conduct and behaviour; once he has attuned our sensitivity to hair-breadth distinctions, it is difficult to ignore such plainer matters.

Why should these things bother us in Congreve's comedies and yet not bother us in Jonson's? After all, Morose is treated a good deal worse than Lady Wishfort is, and Truewit's notion of cruelty is more refined than Mirabell's. One answer may be that in *Epicoene* there seem to be few suggestions that the behaviour of Truewit should be seen as exemplary. He wins out at the end of the play because of his *wit*, which, like that of Brainworm in *Every Man In His Humour* (v. iii. 113) or of Face in *The Alchemist* (v. v. 150), is simply a matter of quick intellectual dexterity; if in these plays, as in real life, such men do win out, they are not necessarily to be seen as patterns for emulation. Dryden evidently took this point; when he called Truewit 'the best character of a gentleman which Ben Jonson ever made',[1] Dryden was not praising him, but rather using Jonson's precedent to justify his own practice of rewarding at the end of his comedies characters who were by no means perfect. Congreve, on the other hand, evidently considered that Jonson's Truewit was a character to be admired, as do Congreve's best critics, the Mueschkes, who declare that for both Jonson and Congreve a Truewit embodied 'the ideal social and intellectual norm of the society of his era'.[2] Under the pressure of Collier's attack on the character of Valentine in *Love for Love*, Congreve somewhat uneasily replied that Valentine was 'a mix'd Character', 'and, as the World goes, he may pass well enough for the best Character

---

[1] Preface to *An Evening's Love*, in *Essays*, ed. Ker, i. 142. (Dryden discusses the character of Truewit more fully in showing how Jonson's notion of a gentleman differs from that of the present age in his 'Defence of the Epilogue; or an Essay on the Dramatic Poetry of the Last Age', *Essays*, i. 174.)

[2] *A New View*, p. 41.

in a Comedy . . .'.[1] Mirabell, however, is not quite the same type as Valentine; as the Mueschkes themselves point out, when writing *The Way of the World* Congreve took pains to modify the character types he had used before; and in his last comedy he presents us with a hero who is *mirable*: wonderful, meet to be admired. Yet Congreve also allows Mirabell to take on the traditional role of the *eiron* of Old Comedy, or of the clever, hardened, high-spirited young trickster of New Comedy, out to get the girl and the money. Comic traditions of considerable antiquity are imperfectly modified to suit the new moral demands of the age; as a result, Mirabell's role veers a little uncomfortably between that of Jonson's Truewit and that of Jane Austen's Mr. Knightley. Perhaps it was only in the larger and subtler form of the novel that the older comic traditions could undergo successful transformation. (In Fielding's early plays the figure of the cheerfully successful rake survives in a fairly pure form; in *Tom Jones* the type is subjected to important modifications.)

Similar problems arise in the case of the play's malevolent characters. These may be observed, for instance, in one of the play's several echoes of *Epicoene* which comes in the fifth act as Mrs. Marwood attempts to convince Lady Wishfort of the intolerable torments of the divorce courts:

Mrs. Marwood. Nay this is nothing; if it wou'd end here, 'twere well. But it must after this be consign'd by the Short-hand Writers to the publick Press; and from thence be transferr'd to the hands, nay into the Throats and Lungs of Hawkers, with Voices more Licentious than the loud *Flounder-man's* or the *Woman* that crys *Grey-pease*; and this you must hear till you are stunn'd; Nay, you must hear nothing else for some days.   (v. i. 229–36)

---

[1] *Amendments of Mr. Collier's False and Imperfect Citations, etc.* (London, 1698), p. 90.

Here it is Truewit's nimble and long-winded cataloguing to Morose of the pains of marriage that comes first to mind; Marwood's deployment of her arguments has the same delighted relentlessness as Truewit's: 'You beginne to sweat, sir? but this is not halfe, i'faith: you may do your pleasure notwithstanding, as I said before, I come not to perswade you' (*Epicoene* II. ii. 86–8). Overlaying this is a memory of another part of *Epicoene*, Morose's account of the terrors of the divorce courts:

> *Morose.* O, no! there is such a noyse i' the court, that they haue frighted mee home, with more violence then I went! such speaking, and counter-speaking, with their seuerall voyces of *citations, appellations, allegations, certificates, attachments, intergatories, references, conuictions,* and *afflictions* indeed, among the Doctors and the Proctors! that the noise here is silence too't! a kind of calme mid-night!   (IV. vii. 13–19)

In imitating Jonson, Congreve makes one significant change: he gives this buoyantly inventive catalogue of torments to a character whom we know is intent upon evil; and by allowing Mrs. Marwood this sudden surge of linguistic energy he manages to prevent us from feeling that this evil is a real and actual threat. Mrs. Marwood momentarily takes on the role of a Truewit, dancing mischievously (not unlike Mirabell himself) about the person of Lady Wishfort. No one until Dickens (we are to hear this voice once more, telling us of Jarndyce and Jarndyce and of the Circumlocution Office) was to achieve so accomplished an imitation of Jonson's style as Congreve does here and elsewhere in the play.[1] Yet Congreve's imitation here has

---

[1] Jonson's influence can be detected in many aspects of the play's plot and phraseology. Kathleen Lynch discusses the influence of *The Devil is an Ass* upon *The Way of the World* in her *The Social Mode of Restoration Comedy* (London and New York, 1926), pp. 192–3, and the Mueschkes (p. 83 n. 4) pertinently recall Truewit's warning to Morose (*Epicoene*, II. ii. 142–3) that 'wise widdowes' are wont to make over their property 'in trust to some

a curiously gratuitous comic effect, and is out of keeping with the spare, tense style which he has created for Mrs. Marwood in other parts of the play ('Indeed Mrs. Engine, is it thus with you?', etc.: III. i. 225 ff.).

We are back at the difficult problem of Congreve's 'artificiality'. In one sense, Mrs. Marwood's talk about the consequences of bringing family scandal into the law courts could be said to be exceedingly realistic: it lets us hear the very street cries of the day, the flounder man and the woman selling '*Grey-pease*'. In another sense the speech could be described as a comic artificiality, an imitation of Jonson inserted without due respect for consistency and context. In a similar fashion, the whole of the fifth act of the play could be said to move, in the manner I have described above, to a practical and 'worldly' conclusion, and in that respect be realistic; or it could just as plausibly be said to move to a Cinderella-conclusion, and in that respect to be artificial. The play turns (we might go on) on the hard, realistic facts of a legacy struggle; yet Millamant's legacy of £12,000 represents a glamorous improvement upon the kind of fortune which a girl of her class and time might seem likely to inherit, and in that sense could be reckoned an artificial element in the play.[1] It is not surprising

friend' before marriage. Many smaller details in the play also awaken memories of Jonson: the notion of the cabal of women, which was to find its culmination in *The School for Scandal*, may derive from the Collegiates of *Epicoene*; Mirabell compares himself to a man in a windmill (II. i. 493–5), as does Morose (v. iii. 61–3); Petulant quarrels in the very accents of Humphrey Wasp (e.g. at III. i. 404–6, and IV. i. 366–70); when he declares he will go off and sleep, Witwoud encourages him, 'Do, rap thy self up like a *Wood-louse* and dream Revenge', just as Clerimont and Truewit have encouraged Sir John Daw when he declared he would go off and be very melancholic: 'As a dog, if I were you, sir IOHN.' 'Or a snaile, or a hog-louse: I would roule my selfe vp for this day, introth, they should not vnwinde me' (II. iv. 140–2). Such details could be multiplied.

[1] John Loftis, *Comedy and Society from Congreve to Fielding* (Stanford, 1959), pp. 46–8.

that the critics have been remarkably divided in their views of *The Way of the World*; for one recent critic (Rose Zimbardo) the most conspicuous feature of the play is that it 'has to do with the "Danger" of medieval romance allegory; it is the hesitance of woman to submit even to the faithful lover';[1] while for another critic (W. H. Van Voris) the most conspicuous feature appears to be Hogarthian realism:

> The seventeenth century had created great clear windows for their elegant town houses, and thanks to Lady Wishfort's decaying gentility and her servant's lie we see their London and smell its stench of open cesspools, decaying garbage in the streets —and death. Outside the poor shiver in hovels of weatherboard. Debtor's prisons are crowded with the starving and diseased.[2]

One will search the play in vain for those long clear windows and that smell of decaying garbage. This view of the play is surely as extreme in its aberrations as was Charles Lamb's view. Lamb emphasized the artificiality of the play in order to defend it against literal-minded criticism. The present tendency, seen (in quite different degrees of subtlety) in the approaches of the Mueschkes, of Kenneth Muir, and of Van Voris, is to praise the comedy as one which deals in a fundamentally realistic way with serious contemporary problems (for the Mueschkes and for Muir, problems concerning marriage; for Van Voris, larger problems of social organization in post-Revolutionary England); and doubtless these readings have been prompted to some extent by the desire to defend the play from the criticism that it is too far removed from real life.

All comedy is of course an amalgam of elements which we may inadequately try to describe as 'realistic' and

---

[1] Rose Zimbardo, *Wycherley's Drama* (New Haven and London, 1965), p. 9.
[2] W. H. Van Voris, *The Cultivated Stance* (London, 1966), p. 139.

'artificial'. In some senses Jonson's comedies could be said to be more 'artificial' than Congreve's; after all, when Congreve said that 'the distance of the Stage requires the Figure represented to be something larger than the Life', he was defending Jonson's characterization of Morose, but defending it a little reluctantly, as his own methods of characterization did not allow for such exaggeration as Jonson's.[1] But to praise (or to condemn) a comedy for being realistic (or artificial) is to risk overlooking the crucial point of interest, which consists in the way in which the play's different elements are reconciled. What is mildly troubling about Congreve's comedies is the reconciliation of these elements. The reluctance of Angelica in *Love for Love* would be perfectly acceptable provided we could be consistently persuaded of the relevance of the conventions of medieval romance allegory; yet the play lives sufficiently in the real world for Lord Orville's objections to this reluctance not to seem critically naïve. Mirabell's treatment of Lady Wishfort is perfectly acceptable so long as we think of the way in which comic protagonists traditionally go about their business in the plays of Plautus or of Lyly; the difficulties arise when we think of Congreve attempting to make his play proof against the charges of Collier and free from 'ill-manners'. The plays hover a little uncomfortably between two worlds. There is plausibility in Van Voris's view that Congreve wanted to deal seriously in his comedies with (amongst other things) the problem of evil in his society, and it is possible to find villains in contemporary history whose actions were quite as black as those of the villains of Congreve's plays (Van Voris asks us, before we condemn Maskwell in *The Double-Dealer*, to remember Robert Young, whose lies and forgeries were good enough to persuade the Privy Council to send the

[1] *William Congreve: Letters and Documents*, ed. Hodges pp. 180-1.

innocent Marlborough to the Tower in 1692).[1] Yet there is surely also a stronger plausibility in the view expressed by Horace Walpole in the mid 1770s that in Congreve's comedies the presence of evil, like that of the other stronger passions, is never really felt:

> We are so pleased with each person, that we wish success to all; and our approbation is so occupied, that our passions cannot be engaged. We even do not believe that a company who seems to meet only to show their wit, can have any other object in view. Their very vices seem affected, only to furnish subject for gaiety. . . . For these reasons, though they are something more, I can scarce allow Congreve's to be true comedies.[2]

These problems, like the other problems which the play presents, might indeed be said to constitute little more than hair-line cracks in what is unquestionably a remarkable comic structure. Discussion of the comedies of Congreve and his contemporaries still has a tendency to run to indignant extremes of panegyric or of hostility; it is necessary to insist both on the quality of the achievement in *The Way of the World* and of the existence in the play of disturbing elements and unresolved technical problems. Possibly they are problems which Congreve might have resolved had he had the spirit to return out of his premature retirement—as Jonson returned out of his premature retirement at the failure of *Catiline* to write *Bartholomew Fair*—and tackle them once again. As it is, *The Way of the World* remains a comedy which, in its very intricacy and accomplishment, continues to reveal to us the difficulty of those technical problems which every writer of comedy must face.

---

[1] Op. cit., pp. 57–8.
[2] 'Thoughts on Comedy', in *The Works of Horatio Walpole, Earl of Orford* (London, 1798), ii. 315–22.

CHAPTER SEVEN

'A Double Capacity': *The Beggar's Opera*

> For the generality of men, a true Modern Life is like a
> true Modern Play, neither Tragedy, Comedy, nor Farce,
> nor one, nor all of these. Every Actor is much better
> known by his having the same Face, than by his keeping
> the same Character: For we change our minds as often as
> they can their parts, & he who was yesterday Cesar, is to
> day Sir J. Daw. So that one might, with much better
> reason, ask the same Question of a Modern Life, that Mr.
> Rich did of a Modern Play; Pray do me the favor, Sir, to
> inform me: Is this your Tragedy or your Comedy?
>
> POPE to CROMWELL, 29 August 1709[1]

I

The Beggar's Opera has had a remarkable stage history, in
respect both of its enduring popularity and of the wide
variety of ways in which it has been interpreted. Its popularity in modern times derives very largely from two famous
and quite different productions of the 1920s. Nigel Playfair's
long-running London production (which in turn set off a
train of critical and scholarly works and small editions of
the plays) was pretty and porcelain, its music (arranged
by Frederick Austen) decorative, sweet, pathetic. Bertolt
Brecht's adaptation, *Die Dreigroschenoper*, presented in
Berlin in 1928, was quite another thing, its caustically
unsentimental tone perfectly conveyed by the music of Kurt
Weil. Neither production could be said to have interpreted
The Beggar's Opera very faithfully, and it is understandable
that Empson should have spoken tartly in his splendid

---

[1] *The Correspondence of Alexander Pope*, ed. George Sherburn (Oxford,
1956), i. 71.

essay on the play in the early thirties: 'It is a fine thing that the play is still popular, however stupidly it is enjoyed.'[1] And yet there has seldom been a period in which *The Beggar's Opera* has not been, in some sense, 'stupidly' enjoyed, and this tendency to provoke a wide range of responses and interpretations is not the least intriguing aspect of the play. Eighteenth-century performances of the play were quite as various as those in modern times. In 1777—to take just one instance—*The Whitehall Evening Post* found occasion to complain with equal tartness of the two productions of *The Beggar's Opera* then running at the two main London theatres; at one house Lucy was being played as high tragedy, at the other she was played as low comedy, and 'we scruple not to pronounce them both wrong'.[2] Not tragedy, not comedy; then what do you call it? In an earlier rehearsal play, Gay had put that question in his very title: *The What D'Ye Call It*. The play defied all categories; it was, said Gay, 'A Tragi-Comi-Pastoral Farce'. There is a well-known letter in which Pope and Gay speak delightedly of the bewildering effect *The What D'Ye Call It* has had upon its audiences. Some of the town, they write, have taken the play as 'a mere jest upon the tragic poets', others have seen it as a satire on the late war; the deaf Mr. Cromwell, hearing none of the words, was much surprised to see the audience laughing at such apparently tragical action; those who came to hiss were so diverted that they forgot the purpose of their visit. The 'common people of the pit and gallery', Pope and Gay go on, 'received it at first with great gravity and sedateness, some few with tears; but after the third day they also took

---

[1] William Empson, '*The Beggar's Opera*', in *Some Versions of Pastoral* (2nd imp., London, 1950), p. 250.

[2] *The Whitehall Evening Post*, Tuesday, 11 November 1777; cited in W. E. Schultz, *Gay's 'Beggar's Opera'* (New Haven and London, 1923), pp. 76–7.

the hint, and have ever since been loud in their clapps'.[1] It was a perfect Scriblerian victory; a victory for what Hugh Kenner has well described as the art of counterfeiting.[2] Counterfeiting is quite different from hoaxing; the puzzlement set up by *The What D'Ye Call It* or *The Beggar's Opera* is of quite a different order from that temporary puzzlement aroused by, let us say, Ireland's *Vortigern*. Even after long familiarity with Gay's work, even after taking 'the hint', one is still likely to feel the variousness of its appeal, its odd ability to be at once ironical and sentimental, risible and grave.

A small cross-section taken from near the end of *The Beggar's Opera* will show how Gay's kind of counterfeiting works, and how complex its effects may be. A writer in the first number of *The Sentimental Magazine* in 1773 observed that the principal difficulty of approaching Gay's work was to know how seriously it was intended, as simplicity and 'the real pathetic' are so intermingled with the humorous and parodic that 'one is at a loss whether to take it as jest or earnest—whether to laugh or cry'. 'Indeed', he went on, after discussing this difficulty in relation to *The Shepherd's Week*,

this effect is also produced in his two dramatic burlesques, the Beggar's Opera and What d'ye call it; for how ludicrous soever the general character of the piece may be, when he comes so near to hanging and shooting [*sic*] in good earnest, the joke ceases; and I have observed the tolling of St. *Pulcre's-bell* received by an audience with as much tragical attention and sympathetic terror as that in Venice Preserved.

The testimony about eighteenth-century audience reaction to the final moments of *The Beggar's Opera* is of some interest; so too is the fact that the writer should turn

---

[1] *The Letters of John Gay*, ed. C. F. Burgess (Oxford, 1966), p. 19 (letter of 3 March 1714/15).

[2] Hugh Kenner, *The Counterfeiters* (Bloomington and London, 1968).

instinctively for his comparison to a similar effect in Otway's *Venice Preserv'd*. For it seems highly probable that Otway's scene was just the one which Gay here intended to burlesque. Pierre's heroic ascent to the scaffold in Act v of *Venice Preserv'd* was one of the most celebrated tragic moments of the Restoration and eighteenth-century stage. As Pierre awaits his execution, the *Passing-bell tolls*; assured by his friend Jaffeir that his death will be honourable— Jaffeir will stab him, then stab himself, at the gallows— Pierre proudly presents himself to his executioners with the measured words, *Come, now I'm ready*. That bell had been gently mocked by Addison in the forty-fourth *Spectator* paper as early as 1711; and the year after the first performance of *The Beggar's Opera* Pope was also to speak dryly of the tolling bell as 'a mechanical help to the Pathetic, not unuseful to the modern writers of Tragedy'.[1] Gay's use of the tolling bell in the last act of *The Beggar's Opera* as Macheath, standing between Polly and Lucy, also awaits Jack Ketch ('Would I might be hanged!') just as clearly mocks this highly popular dramatic device. Suddenly confronted with four more wives, with a child apiece, Macheath reaches desperately for the dignity of Pierre's own phrase: '*Here—tell the Sheriffs officers I am ready.*' (An extra relish was given to the allusion by the fact that Walker, the actor playing Macheath in the original production at Lincoln's Inn Fields, had also played Pierre at the same theatre a few weeks earlier.)[2] No gallows joke, I suppose, is likely to be simple in its effects; that this one should compel an audience to 'tragical attention and sympathetic terror' does suggest, however, an abnormal emotional complexity, an abnormal success at the counterfeiter's art. 'Sublimity,'

---

[1] *The Dunciad* (1729), ii. 220 n.
[2] *The London Stage, 1660–1800*, ed. Emmett L. Avery; Part 2: *1700–29* (Carbondale, Illinois, 1960), p. 950.

wrote Goldsmith, 'if carried to an exalted height, approaches burlesque....'[1] Gay's art reverses the process: his burlesque, carried to an exalted height, approaches sublimity.

Gay's counterfeiting is different not only from mere hoaxing but also from mere literary parody and ridicule. His style of burlesque is quite unlike that of Buckingham. 'Our Poets make us laugh at Tragoedy / And with their Comedies they make us cry', Buckingham had written in the prologue to *The Rehearsal*, stating what was to become the commonest of eighteenth-century theatrical jokes, that it was impossible nowadays to tell comedy and tragedy apart. Behind this joke lay the neo-classical premiss that comedy and tragedy ought to be firmly kept apart; the premiss of Goldsmith's *Essay on the Theatre*, in which he complains that comedy and tragedy, traditionally kept in 'different channels', had lately encroached upon each other's provinces. Gay converts a stock joke into a new art-form. '*The whole Art of* Tragi-Comi-Pastoral Farce', he wrote in his Preface to *The What D'Ye Call It*, '*lies in interweaving the several kinds of the Drama with each other, so that they cannot be distinguished or separated.*' And in his 'interweaving' of the dramatic kinds Gay gently challenges the old neo-classical premiss that insists that the kinds be kept pure and distinct. In *The Beggar's Opera* heroic tragedy, Italian opera, pastoral, popular ballads, and sentimental comedy merge bizarrely together, continually awakening ironical memories of other kinds of literary experience yet nevertheless forming a whole which is in some ways curiously life-like. 'By the assumed licence of the mock-heroic style', Hazlitt wrote perceptively, Gay 'has enabled himself to *do justice to nature*'.[2]

---

[1] 'An Enquiry into the Present State of Polite Learning in Europe', in *The Collected Works of Oliver Goldsmith*, ed. Arthur Friedman (Oxford, 1966), i. 288.

[2] *The Complete Works of William Hazlitt*, ed. P. P. Howe, after the edition of A. R. Waller and Arnold Glover (London and Toronto, 1930), iv. 65.

What is 'natural', perhaps, is the sense which Gay stimulates of the manifold possible ways of looking at any set of actions: as in life itself, an act may be heroic, or laughable, or sad; the plays are unclassifiable, open-ended. And in this respect they may strike us as being peculiarly modern.

The challenge to neo-classical principles was also being made about this time by other and more serious campaigners. Steele had argued in *Tatler* 172 that one really ought to be able to write tragedy not only about 'the history of princes, and persons who act in high spheres', but also about 'such adventures as befall persons not elevated above the common level'. The common man is potentially as much of a tragic figure as is the prince. It is little wonder that eighteenth-century audiences were confused as to the proper way of responding to the echoes of *Venice Preserv'd* as Macheath went to the gallows at the end of *The Beggar's Opera*, for such echoes of heroic tragedy were a common device in the new bourgeois tragedy. Only three years after the first performance of *The Beggar's Opera*, George Lillo in the final act of *The London Merchant* was to imitate closely the final act of *Venice Preserv'd*: as George Barnwell awaits his execution at the scaffold, the passing bell tolls once more, and Barnwell, like Macheath, prepares to meet his death with a half-quotation from Otway on his lips: 'I am summoned to my fate. . . . *Tell 'em I'm ready.*' The fate of a London prentice, Lillo implies, should hold the same poignancy for us as the fate of Macbeth or Faustus or Pierre. If a prentice may take on heroic stature, why may not a highwayman too? In his Preface to *The What D'Ye Call It* Gay had gravely repeated the arguments of the propagandists for the new bourgeois tragedy. To the 'objection' that the sentiments of the play are '*not Tragical, because they are those of the lowest country people*', he answered:

'. . . *that the sentiments of Princes and clowns have not in reality that difference which they seem to have: their thoughts are almost the same, and they only differ as the same thought is attended with a meanness or pomp of diction, or receive a different light from the circumstances each Character is conversant with.*' Gay puts a new ironical edge on the sentimentalists' proposition. It is only 'circumstances' and the artificial conventions of 'diction' (high style for princes, low style for clowns) which disguise the basic truth that all men are alike, that those in low life are no worse than those in high, that those in high life are no better than those in low. All men may therefore be seen as heroes; or, if you prefer, all men may therefore be seen as rogues. And so often in Gay's work, the question is left open: we may look at it which way we please. Yet what we cannot forget—and the fact is important to an understanding of *The Beggar's Opera*—is the general sense of the interchangeability of men. Despite all appearances, one man will turn out to be much the same as another.

II

The Beggar's Opera, wrote Pope, was 'a piece of Satire which hit all tastes and degrees of men, from those of the highest Quality to the very Rabble'.[1] All classes and all men come within the arc of its satire; no one is left unscathed. Yet it is the method of Gay's irony to keep maintaining the illusion that this is not so at all; that although things are in a bad way in this society there must surely be exceptions some-where to the general rule; someone must be kind, someone must be honest, someone must be heroic. Throughout the play Gay keeps suggesting possible exceptions to the general rule of bourgeois possessiveness and self-interest, possible avenues of romantic freedom and escape, possible

[1] *The Dunciad* (1729), iii. 326 n.

evidence of a primitive honestry; only regretfully, ironically, to dismiss such possibilities, to shut off the avenues and to reject the evidence as we approach more nearly.

The method is seen at its broadest in the opening song of the play:

> *Through all the employments of life*
> *Each neighbour abuses his brother;*
> *Whore and Rogue they call Husband and Wife:*
> *All professions be-rogue one another.*
> *The Priest calls the Lawyer a cheat,*
> *The lawyer be-knaves the Divine;*
> *And the Statesman, because he's so great,*
> *Thinks his trade as honest as mine.*

Peachum's song pictures a society in which all men are reduced to a common level: husbands and wives stand on the same footing as rogues and whores; priests and lawyers are as bad as each other; all men are 'brothers' in that they are all united in knavery. Yet there is one exception to this cheerless general rule, one honest man in this corrupt society: Peachum. And Peachum's 'trade' is that of an informer and receiver of stolen goods. Peachum explains how his trade might be said to be honest: 'A Lawyer is an honest employment, so is mine. Like me too he acts in a double capacity, both against Rogues and for 'em; for 'tis but fitting that we should protect and encourage Cheats, since we live by 'em.' 'A double capacity', Peachum implies, is twice as useful as a single one; the phrase suggests a sophisticated professional versatility, like that of the lawyer, who can now prosecute, now defend, using the law as a rapier or as a shield as the need arises. No one needs to be told that Peachum's 'capacity' is in fact that of the double agent, that he is as great a rogue as everyone else in his society. The phrase 'double capacity' might also be said to describe the way in which Gay's own irony works, saying one thing and implying another, shaping a double picture of Peachum and (in turn) of every other character in the play. The ironical method in this opening passage is enjoyably broad and easy; no one could be fooled by Peachum. Yet it is worth watching even at this stage of the play how Gay creates an awareness that things may be seen in a multiplicity of ways. Here is how Peachum resolves to secure the release from Newgate of some female members of the gang: 'I love to let the women scape. A good sportsman always lets the Hen-Partridges fly, because the breed of the game depends upon them. Besides, here the Law allows us no reward; there is nothing to be got by the death of women —except our wives.' Sportsman's heartiness, old-fashioned gallantry to the ladies, and financial shrewdness are nicely blended. The passage invites us to see Peachum as softhearted, and to see him as callous; to see women as objects of chivalry, and to see them as mere 'game'; to see them as being of value, because they are breeders, and as being of no value, for the law allows no reward for information against them. Everything depends upon your viewpoint. Like hen-partridges the women are allowed to escape, but like hen-partridges they are at the same time captive within the lord's domain; the image of the bird which is apparently free but in fact captive runs throughout the play. Then the perspective shifts once more; women are praised, in a barbed phrase, as the educators of men and their rewarders ('We and the surgeons are more beholden to women than all the professions beside'), then instantly condemned as the seducers of men:

> *'Tis woman that seduces all mankind,*
> *By her we first were taught the wheedling arts:*
> *Her very eyes can cheat; when most she's kind,*
> *She tricks us of our money with our hearts.*

> *For her, like Wolves by night we roam for prey,*
> *And practise ev'ry fraud to bribe her charms;*
> *For suits of love, like law, are won by pay,*
> *And Beauty must be fee'd into our arms.*

It is not the men who trap the women—thus runs the argument of Filch's song—but rather the women who trap the men, as they have done since the time of Eve, the archetypal wheedler and betrayer. The men are betrayed by the softness of their hearts. The betrayal is not that the women are unfaithful, but that they demand cash. Hence men are turned into predatory '*Wolves*', against their better natures. What should be noticed is the revolution of images here, as men and women take it in turns to be hungry predators and innocent victims, wolves and partridges, confusing in our minds the notion of who is hunting whom, but suggesting obliquely that everyone may be seen as acting in a double capacity, that no one is simply a hunter or simply a prey, that society is at war with itself, and that that war is at its most deadly in the relationship between the sexes. Tempering such suggestions is the gaiety of the dramatic moment; the predominant mood is set by the light, darting melody to which the song is set. The final effect is thus one of incongruity : the incongruity of a sharpster protesting that he had been undone, yet at the same time educated, by the ladies; the incongruity of words and music, as this unsettling vision of society is unfolded with such gay charm.

This ironic revolution of images continues throughout the play; it is typical of Gay's method that within one song (Air XLV) he should have Lockit picturing himself first as a gudgeon, the 'easy prey' of his treacherous daughter, next as a trapper, catching one innocent bird (Macheath) with another unwitting decoy (Lucy). It is in the case of Macheath and Polly that this confusion of role is most delicately suggested; and once again the predominant images are those of hunter and hunted. Mrs. Peachum's wish is to save Macheath from the predatory company of lords and gentlemen; 'he should leave them to prey upon one another.' Yet it is more logical (as Samuel Butler had suggested) to see a highwayman himself as an animal of prey: 'Aristotle held him to be but a kind of huntsman; but our sages of the law account him rather a beast of prey, and will not allow his game to be legal by the forest law.'[1] We are to learn in due course (III. ii) that the image is an apt one for Macheath, who keeps company with lords and gentlemen in their gaming-houses merely so as to know who is worth setting upon on the road. And yet (as Empson's analysis makes clear) there is also the suggestion that Macheath may indeed be a victim, in his relationship with Polly:

I know as well as any of the fine ladies [says Polly] how to make the most of my self and of my man too. A woman knows how to be mercenary, though she hath never been in a court or at an assembly. We have it in our natures, papa. If I allow captain *Macheath* some trifling liberties, I have this watch and other visible marks of his favour to show for it.

For a new wife to claim that she knows how 'to make the most' of her husband suggests that she has a concern for advancing him in the world. What Polly has in fact been doing (the syntax glides us demurely over the point) is getting what she can out of her husband in order to line her own pockets.

The imagery of Polly's songs continues the doubt as to who is hunting whom:

> *I, like a ship in storms, was tost;*
> *Yet afraid to put in to Land;*
> *For seiz'd in the port the vessel's lost,*
> *Whose treasure is contreband.*

[1] Samuel Butler, *Characters and Passages from Note-Books*, ed. A. R. Waller (Cambridge, 1908), p. 227.

The Waves are laid,
My duty's paid.
O joy beyond expression!
Thus, safe a-shore,
I ask no more,
My all is in my possession.

'Duty' is both a tax, and a moral obligation; the word chimes ironically throughout the play. For other characters than Polly, it seems, 'duty' is something one owes to oneself, and is closely connected with the idea of self-interest. 'If she will not know her duty,' says her mother, 'we know ours'; the duty is to hang Macheath before he hangs them. For the ladies of the town, love is the 'duty' which they owe to themselves in their youth (Air XXII); the gang go 'upon duty' on the heath in order to make themselves rich. Polly's duty, on the other hand, appears to be directed outwards; there seems to be something endearingly old-fashioned about her ideas of social responsibility. And yet the song also pictures Polly as a smuggler; the contraband 'treasure' is Macheath (Gay has given a specific sense to the colloquial phrase, 'you treasure'), who is reduced to a mere possession which Polly is now free to enjoy. She is free, Macheath is a mere possession; the highwayman, whose job it is to capture other people's treasure, is himself captured by Pirate Polly. The point is again made with a sweet obliqueness (quite lost in Brecht's 'Pirate Jenny'), the whole conceit of the song apparently arising out of an innocent imitation of a favourite operatic simile ('the ship') which the Beggar has warned us earlier he will introduce by way of heightening. The adventurer and the turtle-dove; such is Polly's double capacity.

It is this controlled confusion of imagery which causes, in turn, our confusion of response as we watch the play. It is perhaps as important that the sentimentality of the play can hold the irony in check as it is the other way about; Brecht's version of the play shows how much is lost by the removal of this sentimental counterweight. There is nothing in *Die Dreigroschenoper* which manages to strike a note quite like this:

> Now I'm a wretch indeed—Methinks I see him already in the cart, sweeter and more lovely than the nosegay in his hand!—I hear the crowd extolling his resolution and intrepidity!—What vollies of sighs are sent from the windows of *Holborn*, that so comely a youth should be brought to disgrace!—I see him at the tree! the whole Circle are in tears!—even Butchers weep!— *Jack Ketch* himself hesitates to perform his duty, and would be glad to lose his fee, by a reprieve.

In 1770 Francis Gentleman, writing in *The Dramatic Censor*, praised this speech for its pathos and simplicity: '. . . the breaks are fine, the sentiments tender, the description lively, all dressed in a naïveté of language, which finds a passage to the heart, by nature's aid alone.'[1] Gay's counterfeiting is such that it is possible to believe that one is watching an orthodox sentimental drama. 'Those cursed Play-books she reads have been her ruin', Mrs. Peachum has said of her daughter, and Polly's speech is a creditable imitation of the way in which the heroines of the play-books deliver themselves. Polly sees life as like a play, and the assumption that underlies her speech is that in real life people will behave as they do in theatres: 'the whole Circle are in tears', butchers will weep and hangmen melt, everyone will wish for a happy ending. Yet this *is* a play which we are watching, and Macheath *will* be saved (just as Polly hopes) by a reprieve; hence for those (like Francis Gentleman) used to the sentimental traditions, the speech seems to work 'by nature's aid alone'.

[1] *The Dramatic Censor* (London, 1770), i. 117. The passage was also admired by Hazlitt: ibid. iv. 65.

Though Gentleman was quick enough to spot particular touches of literary parody throughout the play, he was evidently prepared to regard certain whole scenes as genuinely pathetic. The first encounter between Polly and Macheath he seemed to regard in this light. 'His reluctance to fly, and her tender resolution to part for a time rather than hazard his safety', he ventured, 'raise delicate feelings.'[1] This scene is, of course, partly intended to ridicule the hackneyed stock scenes of parting lovers; but there is some kind of justification for Gentleman's remarks: certainly the parody is not forced upon us in the way it had been in Cibber's *The Comical Lovers* or as it was to be in the equally ludicrous parting scene in Sheridan's *The Critic*. Such concealment of the parodic tactics heightens the whole scene between Polly and Macheath. '*Were I laid on* Greenland's *coast*' pictures an idyllic lovers' escape, in the style of 'Come live with me and be my love' or 'If you were the only girl in the world,' but is actually—as Empson pointed out— a reply to a question about transportation. And at least some members of the audience must have recalled the last time they had heard that tune on stage, in Farquhar's *The Recruiting Officer*, where both words and context were very different; what Kite and his recruits were celebrating there was their proposed escape from the very domestic ties in which Macheath is now entangling himself:

> We all shall lead more happy lives
> By getting rid of brats and wives,
> That scold and brawl both night and day—
> Over the hills and far away.

The total effect is—as Boswell remarked of another song earlier in the play—'at once . . . painful and ridiculous'.[2]

[1] *The Dramatic Censor*, i. 117–18.
[2] *Boswell's Life of Johnson*, ed. G. B. Hill, rev. L. F. Powell (Oxford, 1934), ii. 368.

Throughout the play each character in turn speaks kindly about his *heart*. Peachum finds that 'it grieves one's heart to take off a great man'; and Mrs. Peachum pleads with him that he be, like herself, not 'too hard-hearted'. Polly's heart, she tells us at once, yields very readily:

> *Though my heart were as frozen as Ice,*
> *At his flame 'twould have melted away.*

And throughout the play Polly's heart, like Lucy's, contrives to melt, bleed, split, burst, and break; 'I know my heart', she modestly remarks. Macheath in his first song announces that 'My heart was so free', but now it is 'riveted' to Polly's; before long, Macheath is in search of the 'free-hearted ladies' of the town. The variation in the depth of the irony means that some of these claims to free- or tender-heartedness are likely to win a temporary credibility. But we can never quite forget the talk of *double capacity* with which the play began; people are likely to play more roles than one; soft hearts may turn to hard; the man who professes himself the lovable victim of society may turn out to be a predator and oppressor. The second act opens with a new mirage of the free life, created by Macheath's gang. Like everyone else, the gang speak well of their hearts: money 'was made for the free-hearted and generous, and where is the injury of taking from another, what he hath not the heart to make use of?' Here is their apologia for the highwayman's profession:

Jemmy Twitcher . . . Why are the laws levell'd at us? are we more dishonest than the rest of mankind? what we win, gentlemen, is our own by the law of arms, and the right of conquest.

Crook-finger'd Jack. Where shall we find such another set of practical philosophers; who to a man are above the fear of Death?

Wat Dreary. Sound men, and true!

Robin of Bagshot. Of try'd courage, and indefatigable industry!

Nimming Ned. Who is there here that would not dye for his friend?

Harry Padington. Who is there here that would betray him for his interest?

Matt of the Mint. Show me a gang of Courtiers that can say as much.

Ben Budge. We are for a just partition of the world, for every man hath a right to enjoy life.

Matt. We retrench the superfluities of mankind. The world is avaricious, and I hate avarice.

This variant of the levellers' plea—beginning with the claim 'we're no worse than our betters', and edging quickly to the larger one, 'we're better than our betters'—has an interesting contemporary analogue: namely, the formal apologias for the merchant's profession commonly found in the new middle-class drama of the day. Steele's Mr. Sealand in *The Conscious Lovers* (IV. ii), and Gay's own Mr. Barter in *The Distress'd Wife* (IV. xvi), champion the merchants against their 'betters', the landed gentry, in very similar style; Lillo's Thorowgood and Trueman in *The London Merchant* were likewise soon to present a panegyric of the merchant as one who relieves nations of their 'useless superfluities', delivering them to other nations in need (III. i). As the merchants justify their occupation, so with equal reasonableness the gang justify theirs. Their defence is attractive, just as Polly's pathos is attractive; and, like Polly, the gang win their admirers: one modern critic seems prepared to take them at their word, considering the passage to represent Gay's own views on the desirability of the even distribution of wealth throughout society.[1]

Yet it is impossible to forget both the context of the passage and the whole ironical movement of the play. For all their fine free-heartedness, for all their Robin Hood air

---

[1] Sven M. Armens, *John Gay, Social Critic* (New York, 1954), p. 56.

of disinterested charity, the gang acts, as everyone else does, in a double capacity. For Macheath, friendship is nowhere to be found save with the gang:

> *The modes of the Court so common are grown,*
> *That a true friend can hardly be met;*
> *Friendship for interest is but a loan,*
> *Which they let out for what they can get.*

Corruption has spread outwards from the Court to infect all society; 'interest'—a complex word of the time, signifying both financial interest and self-interest of the kind spoken of by Hobbes[1]—rules everywhere. But Macheath clings to the one exception to the general rule: 'But we, gentlemen, have still honour enough to break through the corruptions of the world.' Yet, to Macheath's astonishment, it is finally a member of the gang, Jemmy Twitcher, who betrays him—'a plain proof that the world is all alike, and that even our Gang can no more trust one another than other people'. Locke in his *Essay Concerning Human Understanding* (Bk. 1, Ch. 2, § 2), discussing whether or not there could be said to exist any innate moral principles, had interested himself particularly in the moral code of highway men. 'Justice and truth are the common ties of society; and therefore even outlaws and robbers, who break with all the world besides, must keep faith and rules of equity amongst themselves; or else they cannot hold together.'[2] Finally Macheath's gang are shown to lack even that faith and those rules of equity; like everyone else, they are governed solely by 'interest'.

Behind the charm and sentiment of the play is a Hobbesian vision of a world dominated by universal interest. And it is with Hobbes in mind that we should look at the

---

[1] For a discussion of some contemporary usages of the word see Felix Raab, *The English Face of Machiavelli* (London and Toronto, 1964), pp. 157–68.

[2] *An Essay Concerning Human Understanding*, ed. A. C. Fraser (Oxford, 1894).

play's central cluster of images, those which compare and contrast human and animal life. Throughout both his dramatic and his non-dramatic work Gay continually glances back and forth between the world of men and the world of beasts, implying continually that that of the beasts is preferable to that of men:

> But is not man to man a prey?
> Beasts kill for hunger, man for pay.
> (Fable X)

> Here *Shock*, the pride of all his kind, is laid;
> Who fawn'd like Man, but n'er like Man betray'd.
> ('Elegy on a Lap-Dog')

This contrast (as we noticed in Chapter Five)[1] is thoroughly traditional to both pastoral and satire, yet in *The Beggar's Opera* it appears to take on a specific coloration from a still-current philosophical debate. Lockit's speech in the third act of the play should be the starting-point here: 'Lions, Wolves, and Vultures don't live together in herds, droves, or flocks.—Of all animals of prey, man is the only sociable one. Every one of us preys upon his neighbour, and yet we herd together.' The background of this well-known speech is worth investigating.

Up until about the middle of the seventeenth century one of the popular 'proofs' of God's benign ordering of the universe was the fact that animals of prey hunted alone or in pairs, while grazing animals and those necessary to man's comfort and well-being grouped themselves together conveniently in herds. Were the predators to move about in herds, remarked Henry Peacham (the author of *The Compleat Gentleman*) in mild alarm in 1622, 'they would undo a whole country'.[2] This 'proof' about the habits of herding

---

[1] See p. 109 n. 1.

[2] Henry Peacham, *The Compleat Gentleman*, ed. Virgil B. Heltzel (New York, 1962), p. 79.

animals and solitary animals was adduced to support a generally optimistic theory about the efficient organization of the human and animal kingdoms, and of the relationship between them. It was a natural corollary of this theory that human beings themselves, who came together in 'herds' to form towns and cities, were to be reckoned more like cows than like wolves, being pacific rather than warlike. Aristotle had put this even more flatteringly: like ants and bees, men come together naturally and for the common good, yet they are by nature superior to those creatures, because of their knowledge of language, of justice, of good and evil.[1] This theory was devastated by Hobbes at the middle of the century. Men do not come naturally together for the common good (Hobbes argued), but rather for a variety of selfish reasons: for honour, dignity, passion, glory, gain. Man is more like a wolf than he is like a cow or a bee. The human community is unique in that it is the only 'herd' which is composed of animals of prey: therefore its laws and government must be powerfully devised and powerfully imposed.[2] Shaftesbury in his various replies to Hobbes tried to attack this proposition; in his 'An Inquiry Concerning Virtue or Merit' in 1699 he refined the old argument about wild animals living on their own and tame ones sheltering together, and in *Sensus Communis:* 'An Essay on the Freedom of Wit and Humour' in 1709 he insisted upon the naturalness and the mutual usefulness and pleasure of human herding: 'If eating and drinking be natural,' he wrote, 'herding is so too. If any appetite or sense be natural, the sense of fellowship is the same.'[3]

Two distinct views of man as a 'sociable animal' were

---

[1] Aristotle, *Politics*, ed. Ernest Barker (Oxford, 1946), I. ii, § 10 (pp. 5–6).

[2] See especially *De Cive*, II. v, § 5; *Leviathan*, ii. 17.

[3] Shaftesbury, 'An Inquiry Concerning Virtue or Merit', in *Characteristics*, ed. John W. Robertson (London, 1900), i. 237–338; '*Sensus Communis:* An Essay on the Freedom of Wit and Humour', in *Characteristics*, i. 74.

therefore current at the time at which Gay wrote *The Beggar's Opera*: the sceptical Hobbesian view, and the more optimistic view of Shaftesbury, which argued that sociability, like the other human passions, was both instinctive and conducive to the common good; that self-interest and social interest might be the same. There is little doubt, I think, that the Hobbesian view pervades *The Beggar's Opera*; but Gay's achievement is to throw up as an ironical alternative the sentimental Shaftesburian view of things, appearing, as it were, to weigh the two social theories judiciously in the balance, hinting that there *might* be exceptions to the general Hobbesian rule. The Peachums and Lockits, the lords and the gamesters of London come together as Hobbes reckoned men always did in cities, out of self-interest and a desire for mutual plunder. 'If you would not be look'd upon as a fool,' says Lockit to his daughter, 'you should never do anything but upon the foot of interest. Those that act otherwise are their own bubbles.' The gamesters are

> Like pikes, lank with hunger, who miss of their ends,
> They bite their companions and prey on their friends.

'Man is a herded animal, and made for Towns and Cities', says one of the characters in Shadwell's *Bury Fair*; and Gay's vision of the city is the same Hobbesian vision as Shadwell had presented in that play: 'So many Pens of Wild Beasts upon two legs, undermining, lying in wait, preying upon, informing against, and hanging one another: A Crowd of Fools, Knaves, Whores, and Hypocrites.' Yet Gay never puts things quite so bluntly. Possibly (he suggests) the dominant passion is not interest but love, which finally conquers all: '*Can love be controul'd by advice?*' Polly sings; 'How the mother is to be pitied who hath handsome daughters!' Mrs. Peachum complains, 'Locks, bolts, bars, and lectures of morality are nothing to them: they break through them all.' But then, by gradual steps, Gay closes off that sentimental possibility. As Empson's fine account of the play demonstrates, Polly's passionate love for Macheath is subtly presented as being as self-interested and destructive as the tradesman's or the criminal's passion for financial advancement; the tightening of the marriage knot can be as deadly as the tightening of the hangman's. In her ardent quest for the sociability of marriage Polly can look like a beast of prey.

To see how Gay gently subverts the sentimental Shaftesburian premiss about the benign workings of the human passions, we may explore a little further the sources and implications of his literary parody in the final scene of the play. The memories of *Venice Preserv'd* in this scene I have already noted. Overlaying these, however, are other memories of another equally famous heroic tragedy. Polly and Lucy, standing imploringly on either side of Macheath, may well (as earlier critics have suggested) have put an audience in mind of Robert Walpole's wife and mistress struggling for the great man's attention, or even conceivably of Handel's two leading sopranos, Cuzzoni and Faustina, to whom the beggar obliquely alludes in the play's introduction. Yet they would also probably have reminded an audience of Dryden's Octavia and Cleopatra, competing in that famous scene in Act III of *All For Love* for the affection of Antony.

> *Which way shall I turn me—how can I decide?*
> *Wives, the day of our death, are as fond as a bride*

is how Macheath expresses the struggle, echoing the words of Antony before him: 'O Dolabella, *which way shall I turn?*' Antony's struggle is expressed in tears and blushes, the simple appearance of the two women being sufficient to draw forth all his instinctive, though conflicting, affections of pity, shame, and love: the scene might be described as heroic-sentimental. Macheath's struggle is very different:

> *One wife is too much for most husbands to hear,*
> *But two at a time there's no mortal can bear.*

Macheath's dilemma is a dry and intellectual one: how do I get out of this fix? In *Spectator* 44—the same number in which he had mocked the stage device of tolling bells— Addison examined other 'Artifices to fill the Minds of an Audience with Terrour' which were then in popular use, and descended with particular and merciless wit upon this very scene in *All For Love*. Dryden's Octavia, it will be remembered, makes her entrance in this scene '*leading* ANTONY's *two little daughters*'. A disconsolate mother with a child in her hand, Addison remarks, is a convenient device to draw compassion from an audience. 'A Modern Writer', he goes on, observing the fact and 'being resolved to double the Distress', introduced a princess on stage leading a couple of children by the hand; this was such a success that a third writer, not to be outdone, resolved to introduce three children, thus scoring an even greater triumph; and, says Addison, that is not all:

> . . . as I am inform'd, a young Gentleman who is fully determin'd to break the most obdurate Hearts, has a Tragedy by him, where the first Person that appears upon the Stage, is an afflicted Widow in her Mourning-Weeds, with half a Dozen fatherless children attending her, like those that usually hang about the Figure of Charity. Thus several Incidents that are beautiful in a good Writer, become ridiculous by falling into the Hands of a bad one.

With the sudden production at the end of *The Beggar's Opera* of four more wives for Macheath—making six in all on stage—all four bearing 'a child a-piece', Gay clinches the same comic point that Addison had made in *The Spectator*. The fallacy which Gay's parody implicitly attacks is not simply that of believing that pathos can be increased mechanically, like troops in a stage-army; it is also the sentimental fallacy of believing that the mere presence of wives and children will reduce us, mechanically, to tears and hugs and blushes. The affections do not operate with quite the happy regularity which Dryden and Shaftesbury, in their different ways, had suggested. There are times when one would rather stick one's head in the hangman's noose than be sociable any longer.

The final escape-route can only be to death, but that 'the taste of the town' will not allow, and Macheath is saved by a reprieve. The last and cruellest irony is that the sentimental passions will not only drive a man to drink and to the gallows, but that they will also rescue him from those final avenues of freedom with an ominous promise of the nuptial bliss which awaits him:

> But think of this maxim, and put off your sorrow,
> The wretch of to-day, may be happy to-morrow.

It is characteristic that the play should close upon such an ambiguous promise of happy days.

Gay's ironical concession to 'the taste of the town' at the end of *The Beggar's Opera* reminded Colley Cibber of Jonson's similar ironical concessiveness in *Bartholomew Fair*,[1] and on this point, as on other points, the two plays are indeed alike. Each uses similar methods of comic levelling and inversion, bringing before us the fact that, despite all evidence to the contrary, all men are alike; were it not for the reprieve, says Gay's Beggar regretfully, his play would have carried a most excellent moral, 'that the lower sort of people have their vices in a degree as well as the rich: And that they are punish'd for them'. Both plays operate on a double level, entertaining their audiences so

---

[1] *An Apology for the Life of Mr. Colley Cibber*, ed. Robert W. Lowe (London, 1889), i. 245.

agreeably that their ironical undercurrents are not always fully discernible. Both plays move genially to their conclusions, with a wry knowledge of the way in which the theatrical public will like events to be resolved. Both plays— but most of all, *The Beggar's Opera*—maintain to the end an element of tease, of take-it-which-way-you-will. In its various and seemingly contradictory ways, for its pathos and its bathos, as a sentimental lollipop and as a terse social fable, *The Beggar's Opera* will no doubt continue to give equal delight. To deceive us so variously and so well is a triumph of the counterfeiter's art.

CHAPTER EIGHT

High and Low Life:
Fielding and the Uses of Inversion

> Behold, the Lord maketh the earth empty, and maketh it
> waste, and turneth it upside down, and scattereth abroad
> the inhabitants thereof. And it shall be, as with the people,
> so with the priest; as with the servant, so with his master;
> as with the maid, so with her mistress; as with the buyer,
> so with the seller; as with the lender, so with the bor-
> rower; as with the taker of usury, so with the giver of
> usury to him. The earth shall be utterly emptied and
> spoiled; for the Lord hath spoken this word.
>
> Isaiah 24: 1–3

I

HOGARTH completed his last print, *Tailpiece, or the Bathos*,
a few months before his death in 1761. In the background
of the picture stand two bare trees, a gibbet, a ruined tower
on which is a clock which has no hands. Falling diagonally
across the picture is an inn-sign of 'The World's End', on
which is depicted the world in flames. Phaeton's chariot
falls from the sky, while on a distant sea one last ship
performs the gentle art of sinking. In the foreground Father
Time breathes his last word: 'Finis'. His scythe, his hour-
glass, and his pipe are all broken; and scattered in front of
him lie a broken bell, a broken column, a broken bottle,
a broken crown, a broken musket, and a broken palette.
A statute of bankruptcy, inscribed 'H. Nature Bankrupt',
and stamped with the seal of a rider on a pale horse, lies
amidst the broken fragments. Beneath it is a play-book
open at its last page, showing the words *Exeunt Omnes*.

The print is likely to remind one of the ending of the fourth book of *The Dunciad*, where, with a similar use of fine detail, Pope presented a similar picture of the ultimate cosmic 'bathos', the ruin of the civilization of his time. Like Hogarth, Pope had depicted his apocalypse in terms of the ending of a play, which leaves the theatre of the world in final darkness and disarray:

> Thy hand, great Anarch! lets the curtain fall;
> And Universal Darkness buries all.

'They showed the age involved in darkness', wrote Dr. Johnson aptly of Pope and Swift.[1] It is always a little surprising to realize that the peace of the Augustans, as Saintsbury cheerfully called it, should have been ruffled by this myth of *fin du monde*, though perhaps a myth of this kind is a natural companion to such a highly systematic myth of order as Pope was at pains to formulate in *An Essay on Man*:

> The least confusion but in one, not all
> That system only, but the Whole must fall.
>
> (Ep. 1, 249–50)

The more elaborate and delicate you imagine the cosmic mechanism to be, the more you may fear the consequences of its slightest derangement. And similarly, perhaps, the stronger and more specific your conception of the ideal society is, the fiercer and darker your castigation of departures from that ideal may be. Certainly it is remarkable that another apocalyptic myth grew up amongst the writers who so deeply admired the age of Augustus; a myth concerning the advent of a new age which parodied, and would finally obliterate, the values of the first, true Augustan age.[2] This myth necessitated an elaborate comparison be-

---

[1] *Lives of the Poets*, ed. G. B. Hill (Oxford, 1905), iii. 61–2.

[2] See Aubrey Williams, *Pope's 'Dunciad'* (London, 1955); James W. Johnson, 'The Meaning of "Augustan"', *J.H.I.*, xix (1958), pp. 507–22.

PLATE 3

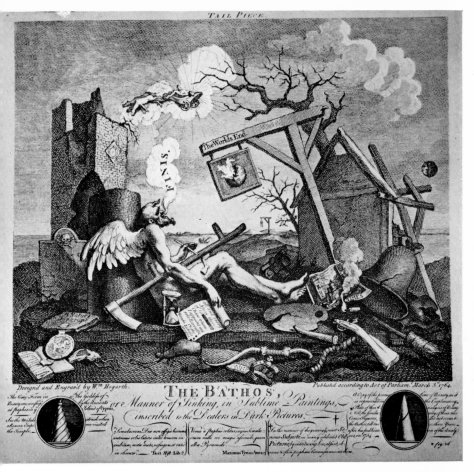

Hogarth's 'Tailpiece, or The Bathos'.

tween the present age and the great age of Roman civilization. The Emperor Augustus was praised by Horace;
George II, christened George Augustus, was praised by
the Reverend Laurence Eusden. The first Augustan age
had produced Virgil and his *Aeneid*; the new Augustan
age had produced Blackmore and his *Creation*. Culture in
that age was patronized by Maecenas; culture in this age
was neglected by Walpole. *The Dunciad* is an extended
ironical celebration of the new Augustan age, in which
Pope sounds a mocking echo to Virgil's messianic notes:

> This, this is He, foretold by ancient rhymes,
> Th'Augustus born to bring Saturnian times.
>   (1728, III. 317–18)

The reign of Augustus Caesar was said to restore the original
harmony of the Golden Age; but the reign of the new
Augustus will bring 'Saturnian times' of anarchy and
disorder.

For Pope and his circle, such anarchy and disorder could
already be seen in the theatre of their day, which—in a
traditional figure—might be taken as an emblem of the
real world. The absurd entertainments presented in the
theatres seemed to reflect the absurdity of the age itself.
Phoebe Clinket, the heroine of *Three Hours After Marriage*,
a comedy by Pope, Gay, and Arbuthnot presented at Drury
Lane in 1717, is busily engaged in writing a tragedy of her
own entitled, appropriately, *The Deluge*; a tragedy which
depicts, with a wonderful confusion of images, the monstrous and inverted world of the flood. Such fare, it is
implied, is well suited to the theatres of the day:

> *Swell'd with a Dropsy, sickly Nature lies,*
> *And melting in a Diabetes, dies . . .*
> *The roaring Seas o'er the tall Woods have broke,*
> *And Whales now perch upon the sturdy Oak.*

N

In the third book of *The Dunciad* Pope gives a similar, though more intensely detailed, picture of the activities of the theatres of his day, whose artificers seem to have brought into being a new and topsy-turvy creation:

> Thence a new world, to Nature's laws unknown,
> Breaks out refulgent, with a heav'n its own:
> Another Cynthia her new journey runs,
> And other planets circle other suns:
> The forests dance, the rivers upward rise,
> Whales sport in woods, and dolphins in the skies;
> And last, to give the whole creation grace,
> Lo! one vast Egg produces human race.   (237–44)

Pope's image of this *new world*—wild, lawless, parodic—brilliantly co-ordinates a number of traditional and contemporary notions. Like the passage from Phoebe Clinket's play, it reaches back to Ovid's account of the deluge in Book One of the *Metamorphoses*, glancing at the same time at Horace's remarks about monstrosities in art (some painters give us a dolphin in the woods, a boar in the flood). At the centre of the image is the idea of the poet as a little god, whose activities imitate, in a humble way, the greater powers of the Creator himself: 'and *a new world* leaps out at his command' (*An Essay on Criticism*, 486).[1] Behind the passage, too, lies a long tradition which we glanced at in Chapter Four, of a fantastic 'new world' discovered in the sun or moon or in a remote area of the earth: a tradition variously represented by Jonson's *News From the New World Discovered in the Moon*, by Cyrano's *L'Autre Monde*, and by Durfey's *Wonders in the Sun*. The image is further sharpened by an implied reference to a topic of some contemporary interest, that of the *pluralité des mondes*. Man was allowed to live in one world and to know one world, Pope

---

[1] On this concept see M. H. Abrams, 'The Poem as Heterocosm', in *The Mirror and the Lamp* (New York, 1953), pp. 272–85.

had written in *An Essay on Man*; that was as far as his
knowledge was permitted to reach. It was for God alone to

> See worlds on worlds compose one universe,
> Observe how system into system runs,
> What other planets circle other suns . . .   (24–6)

What has happened in the theatres can happen in society at
large. Man may presumptuously reject the old world in
which God has placed him, and create for himself a new
world which parodies the old, and follows its own unnatural
laws. What looks like creation turns out to be apocalypse.

How seriously Pope and his group believed in all this it
is impossible to tell. There is an obvious playfulness about
the way in which the apocalyptic ideas are handled, an
obvious enjoyment in the use of such lavish hyperbole, yet
the vision is far from comic. It is implied, as in satire it
traditionally is implied, that things are unlikely ever to
improve. The comic artist, as a rule, lets you know that the
chaos is likely to settle a bit in the course of time. The
satirist, as a rule, lets you know that it's no good: all we
can do is sit about lamenting, inveighing, possibly even
joking, but always waiting for the end. The distinction is
one which may be clarified as we move from the work of
the Scriblerians to that of Henry Fielding.

II

Fielding came to London in 1727, the year of George
Augustus's coronation. Pope, Swift, and Gay were at the
height of their powers: *Gulliver's Travels* had been published
the year before, and Pope was at work on *The Dunciad*,
which was published in May of the following year; Gay
was busy writing *The Beggar's Opera*, which was to open at
Lincoln's Inn Fields just a fortnight before Fielding's own
first play, *Love in Several Masques*, was presented at Drury

Lane in February 1728. Gay's opera, Fielding confessed, 'engrosses the whole talk and admiration of the town'.[1] In March of 1728 another Scriblerian work was to appear: *Peri Bathous*, the mock 'Art of Sinking in Poetry', written as early as 1713/14 by Pope, Swift, Gay, Parnell, Oxford, and Arbuthnot, and now rewritten almost entirely by Pope, was published in the third volume of Pope's and Swift's *Miscellanies*. It is scarcely surprising that a young writer just up from the West Country and barely into his twenties should have found the influence of Pope, Swift, Gay, and their circle quite irresistible, and that he should soon be writing under the name of Scriblerus Secundus.

From this older generation of writers Fielding learnt many of the tactics of irony and of satire. From them, too, he picked up a fashionable way of lamenting the times. We live (he declared in one of his poems) in 'no Augustan age';[2] rather, Fielding often implied, it is an age which seems about to disintegrate in farcical disorder. One theme in particular strongly caught Fielding's imagination. Throughout the work of the Scriblerians there recurs, with countless variations, the notion of a ludicrous and sometimes tragic merger of the 'high' and the 'low'. The merger can occur in literature, where (as *Peri Bathous* had shown) the high style is in constant danger of collapsing into the low; it can occur in education—the boast of the pedants in *The Dunciad* is that they bring 'to one dead level ev'ry mind'— it can occur in society as a whole: one of the 'great ends' of Dullness, Pope wrote, was to blot out 'the distinctions between high and low in society'.[3] The levelling of high and low becomes, too, one of the most persistent ideas in Fielding's work, yet with a significant difference of emphasis.

[1] Preface to *Love in Several Masques*, in *Works*, ed. Henley, *Plays and Poems*, i. 9.

[2] 'Of True Greatness', in *Works*, ed. Henley, *Plays and Poems*, v. 255.

[3] *The Dunciad* (1742), IV. 268; 14 n.

As time goes by Fielding gradually converts the Tory satirists' despondent myth of a civilization falling to ruins to more optimistic comic ends; his mood becomes, on the whole, lighter and more amiable, and the levelling tends to be seen not with the savage energy of a satirist who proclaims the approach of the end of the world, but with the gentleness of a comic artist who reminds us of the artificiality of such distinctions in the first place.

The conversion of the idea does not occur all at once. *Tom Thumb*, one of Fielding's earliest and best-known plays (April 1730, revised and enlarged March 1731) is still very much under the Scriblerian spell. 'Tragedy', wrote Fielding in the Preface of 1731, 'hath of all writings the greatest share in the bathos, which is the profound of Scriblerus.' Yet Fielding goes a step further than the Scriblerians, literalizing their metaphor and giving us, instead of the expected herculean hero of 'high' tragedy, the lowest hero ever to walk the English stage. One wonders if Fielding remembered Dryden's observations about the difficulty of bringing heroic literature to the stage: that 'the prowess of Achilles or Aeneas would appear ridiculous in our dwarf heroes of the theatre';[1] or Addison's ridicule, in *Spectator* 42, of the popular stage conventions of heroic tragedy: 'The ordinary Method of making an Heroe, is to clap a huge Plume of Feathers upon his Head, which rises so very high, that there is often a greater Length from his Chin to the Top of his Head, than to the Sole of his Foot. One would believe, that we thought a great Man and a tall Man the same thing.' Like Addison, Fielding brings into ironic confusion the literal and metaphorical meanings of 'great', 'high', and 'low'. The joke kept playing in Fielding's mind; years later in his 'Modern Glossary' (*Covent Garden Journal*, No. 4) he was to define the word 'Great' as follows:

[1] 'Dedication to the Aeneis', *Essays*, ed. W. P. Ker (Oxford, 1900), ii. 161.

'Applied to a Thing, Signifies Bigness; when to a Man, Often Littleness or Meanness'; at a time when Robert Walpole was popularly known as 'the Great', everyone knew what the point of the joke was. In *Tom Thumb* Fielding does not merely ridicule the conventions of heroic tragedy in the way Buckingham had done sixty years before; he implies also that the contemporary uncertainty on theatrical matters may be paralleled by our uncertainty on moral and political matters; in each case we have not sufficiently considered the true meaning of greatness: hence on the theatrical stage and on the stage of public life a dwarf may pass as a hero. Thus the images of wild cosmic turbulence and disaster in *Tom Thumb* have suggestions beyond their immediate point of parody, for they serve as fitting emblems of the actual confusion of the times:

> *Noodle.* Sure, Nature means to break her solid chain,
> Or else unfix the world, and in a rage
> To hurl it from its axletree and hinges;
> All things are so confus'd . . . (II. x)

But although the play has such implications as these, Fielding's use of the apocalyptic myth differs from Pope's even at this stage in that it remains fundamentally genial and amusing. Swift—who, if Dr. Johnson is to be believed, 'stubbornly resisted any tendency to laughter' throughout his life—was reported to have laughed outright on seeing the play.[1] Later, in his Preface to *Joseph Andrews*, Fielding was to reject as 'monstrous and unnatural' the simple inversion device on which *Tom Thumb* and some of his other plays rest—'appropriating the manners of the highest to the lowest, or *è converso*'; yet he pleaded in favour of this burlesque mode its power of arousing laughter, sweetness, good humour, and benevolence. If, as Fielding argued,

---

[1] *Lives of the Poets*, ed. Hill, iii. 56; Laetitia Pilkington, *Memoirs* (1754), iii. 155.

burlesque was not the same thing as true comedy, it was
nevertheless closer to comedy than it was to satire, being
designed not to unsettle and disturb but primarily to amuse
and entertain.

Fielding's burlesque plays often depict society in a state
of collapse. In ridiculing the popular theatrical entertainments of the day Fielding, like Pope, was quick to bring
out the occasional unintentional appropriateness of subject-
matter of such plays. In *Tumble-Down Dick* in April 1736,
for instance, Fielding ridiculed John Rich's pantomime
The Fall of Phaeton, highlighting the aptness of the theme
which Rich had chosen: the fall of Phaeton presaged the
end of the world; Rich's own theatrical nonsense seemed
to have 'turned all nature topsy-turvy', and seemed also
to presage some final cataclysm; such scenes as Rich depicted were fitting emblems and portents of the age. Some
weeks earlier in *Pasquin* Fielding had brought out even more
explicitly the symbolic relationship which Rich's entertainments bore to the age. The second half of *Pasquin*
presents the rehearsal of a tragedy called *The Life and Death
of Common Sense*. Rich's shows at Covent Garden are once
more held up to ridicule; the play-within-the-play reaches
its climax with the invasion from Europe of Queen Ignorance with her troupe of 'singers, fiddlers, tumblers, and
rope-dancers', and with her assassination of the native
Queen Common-Sense. As Common-Sense expires she
utters her last prophecy, that the world will now be turned
upside-down:

> Henceforth all things shall topsy-turvy turn;
> Physic shall kill, and Law enslave the world;
> Cits shall turn beaux, and taste Italian songs,
> While courtiers are stock-jobbing in the city.
> Places, requiring learning and great parts,
> Henceforth shall all be hustled in a hat,

> And drawn by men deficient in them both.
> Statesmen—but oh! cold death will let me say
> No more—and you must guess *et caetera*.　　[*Dies*

Like *The Dunciad, Pasquin* portrays a widespread and ludicrous series of reversals in human relationships, beginning inside the theatres and radiating out into society at large; it is the final 'bathos', the sinking of the social order, the blotting out of 'distinctions between high and low in society'. Yet although the debt to Pope is clear enough in passages such as these, it is equally clear that Fielding is once again using the apocalyptic myth in a significantly different way. *Pasquin* does not end in universal darkness but instead with a rolling back of the clouds. The ghost of Queen Common-Sense revives:

> The coast is clear, and to her native realms
> Pale Ignorance with all her host is fled.

The ending of *The Dunciad* is the traditional ending of satire: we are shown the world falling in ruins about our ears, and are offered no comfort or relief, but are permitted to hear only the bitter protests of the world's solitary honest man. The ending of *Pasquin*, on the other hand, is the ending traditional to comedy: though the world seems to be falling in ruins about our ears, it turns out, miraculously that things are not as confused as they look, and common sense finally triumphs over the forces of disorder.

A play written some years earlier, *The Author's Farce* (March 1730, revised 1734), must serve as a final example of Fielding's methods of inversion in this period, and of his way of moving from satire into comedy; this time we are likely to be reminded not only of the work of Pope but also of that of Ben Jonson. *The Author's Farce* is about a struggling writer named Luckless, who is in debt to his landlady, in love with his landlady's daughter, and unsuccessful in his attempts to sell his plays to the theatre managers. His friend Witmore tells him that the fault lies not with him but with the age. In this age, says Witmore, values are inverted:

> But now, when party and prejudice carry all before them, when learning is decried, wit not understood, when the theatres are puppet-shows and the comediens are ballad singers, when fools lead the town would a man think to thrive by his wit? If you must write, write nonsense, write operas, write entertainments, write *Hurlothrumbos*, set up an *Oratory* and preach nonsense, and you may meet with encouragement enough. If you would receive applause, deserve to receive sentence at the Old Bailey; and if you would ride in your coach, deserve to ride in a cart.

Ben Jonson, who often spoke of his own age in somewhat similar terms, implied in *Bartholomew Fair* what Witmore implies here: that theatrical nonsense is all that such an age deserves to get. Luckless writes a puppet-play about just that: nonsense. The scene is the Court of Nonsense, situated in a kind of Lucianic underworld; the presiding Goddess of Nonsense is visited by a number of figures— a Poet and a Bookseller, Punch and Judy, Signior Opera, Don Tragedio, Sir Farcical Comic, and Mrs. Novel—who report on the progress of cultural affairs in the other world. 'My Lord Mayor has shortened the time of Bartholomew Fair in Smithfield,' announces the Poet, 'and so they are resolved to keep it all the year round at the other end of the town.' In *Bartholomew Fair* Jonson had suggested that the mischievous, Saturnalian values of Smithfield were spreading across London, infecting the groundlings at the Hope Theatre on the Bankside. Pope may have recalled Jonson's play as he ironically celebrated in *The Dunciad* the progress of 'the Smithfield Muses to the ear of Kings', the triumphant extension of the unruly holiday entertainments of Smithfield beyond their natural time and place to invade 'the theatres of Covent-Garden, Lincolns-inn-Fields, and the Haymarket, to be the reigning Pleasures of the Court and Town'.[1] *The Pleasures of the Town* is the title of Luckless's play; Fielding's echo of Pope's phrase shows how close to *The Dunciad* he was working. Like Pope and like Jonson, Fielding dramatizes the threat of a kind of perpetual Saturnalia; like them, he pictures a world in which true drama has had to give way to puppet-shows, in which the role of the 'master-poet' has been usurped by the poetaster, a disordered world which has been left to the mercy of noise and nonsense.

Such at least are Fielding's evident intentions, but *The Author's Farce*, like Fielding's other dramatic burlesques, turns out finally to be a good-natured romp. The play's satirical intentions are mild, and ultimately somewhat muddled. Though the present age, we are told, is one which 'would allow Tom Durfey a better poet than Congreve or Wycherley', Fielding never makes it clear whether Luckless is to be regarded as a Durfey or as a Congreve; if, as it seems, he is a mere hack like Durfey, then it is impossible to feel indignant over the initial rejection of his work by the managers of the theatres or over the later interruption of *The Pleasures of the Town* by a character named Murdertext, who demands, like Zeal-of-the-Land Busy and with equal lack of success, that the show must stop.[2] Fielding was never really able to regard scribblers fiercely as a social menace in the way that Jonson and Pope evidently did, and *The Author's Farce* is written not so much out of satirical con-

---

[1] *The Dunciad* (1729), I. 2 n. The relationship between Fielding's plays and the fourth book of *The Dunciad* is explored by George Sherburn in 'The *Dunciad*, Book Four', *Studies in English*, Department of English, University of Texas (1944), pp. 174–90.

[2] It is to Jonson's credit that he keeps a similar contradiction well concealed at the end of *Bartholomew Fair*; he holds no brief for the kind of puppet-show which Busy wants to stop.

tempt as out of a more tolerant and compassionate interest in the difficulties of surviving at all in Grub Street: hence the sympathetic and almost Dickensian scenes with Dash and Blotpage, Quibble and Scarecrow in the house of Mr. Bookweight. And it is significant that *The Author's Farce*, like *Pasquin*, does not end in lamentation over the darkness of the age, but moves instead into lavish and wholesale farce. Though the transition from satire to farce has none of the fine control which Jonson shows in *Bartholomew Fair*, Fielding's confidence once he has actually reached that final mode shows clearly where his real skills lay, not in satire but in the more exuberant traditions of stage comedy. The comic resolution of *The Author's Farce* anticipates the comic resolution of *Joseph Andrews*; in each case the final rapid sequence of accidents and coincidences does not so much suggest that life is an absurd farce as that life is watched over by a benign providence which will finally set straight all confusions, bringing rewards to the innocent and luck to the luckless.

Even at this early stage in Fielding's career, then, his work shows a significantly different emphasis from that of Pope and his fellow-Scriblerians; and the differences become more apparent when, after the Licensing Act of 1737, Fielding turns his attention to the longer and more complex form of the novel, gradually abandoning his favourite tactics of burlesque inversion. In his novels Fielding continues to depict society in a state of fluidity in which 'the distinctions between high and low' have been dissolved, in which unexpected social reversals and equations occur, yet his art now becomes even more decisively comic in nature. Possibly we may see how and why these changes occur in Fielding's work if we dwell a little longer on the double theme which (to apply in a new context Frank Kermode's conveniently ambiguous phrase) might best be described as his *sense of an ending*.

III

'Throughout the whole piece', Gay's Beggar had declared at the end of his opera, 'you may observe such a similitude of manners in high and low life, that it is difficult to determine whether (in the fashionable vices) the fine gentlemen imitate the gentlemen of the road, or the gentlemen of the road the fine gentlemen.' The Beggar's statement is the last, ironical closing of the circle, the final suggestion that folly and 'interest' are everywhere, and that we must not look for exceptions. It is possible to imagine a fastidious objection to irony which is as universal as Gay's is here. 'Unless there is something about which the author is never ironical,' C. S. Lewis wrote once (defending Jane Austen against the charge of being over-clever at her characters' expense), 'there can be no true irony in the work. "Total irony"—irony about everything—frustrates itself and becomes insipid.'[1] If you show that low life and high life are each in the same catastrophic state and allow your irony to drift on an arc of 360 degrees, what then do you finally believe in? George Orwell made this objection against Swift's irony when discussing *Gulliver's Travels*:

At the end of the book, as typical specimens of human folly and viciousness, Swift names 'a Lawyer, a Pickpocket, a Colonel, a Fool, a Lord, a Gamester, a Politician, a Whoremaster, a Physician, an Evidence, a Suborner, an Attorney, a Traitor, or the like'. One sees here the irresponsible violence of the powerless. The list lumps together those who break the conventional code, and those who keep it. For instance, if you automatically condemn a colonel, as such, on what grounds do you condemn a traitor? Or again, if you want to suppress pickpockets, you must have laws, which means that you must have lawyers.[2]

[1] C. S. Lewis, 'A Note on Jane Austen', *Essays in Criticism*, iv (1954), p. 370.

[2] 'Politics vs. Literature', *The Collected Essays of George Orwell* (London, 1961), p. 390 n. 1.

Tory anarchism was what Orwell called this in Swift: irony which ranged indiscriminately across society from top to bottom, devastating both high and low, both law-makers and law-breakers.

It is possible that Fielding came to feel some such discomfort as this with the 'total irony' of Swift and Gay. Certainly when he imitates their ironic style in his novels Fielding is careful to show us not simply that society is in a bad way but also that this state of affairs is curable, and that there are people and institutions to be excepted from the total sweep of ironic condemnation. One might say that Fielding is more obviously concerned with the social responsibility of the ironic writer, with the dangers of his appearing to laugh at everything. *Jonathan Wild* shows the main points of departure well, being, as it is, so obviously influenced by the ironic methods of *The Beggar's Opera*. Fielding's Count speaks as Gay's Beggar had done: 'It is needless to particularize in every instance,' he declares, 'in all we shall find that there is a nearer connexion between high life and low life than is generally imagined, and that a highwayman is entitled to more favour with the great than he usually meets with.' Yet although Fielding invites us to identify the conduct of Walpole the Prime Minister with that of Wild the master criminal (the identification was a popular one at the time)[1] he does not close the circle entirely: there is an area of society over which his irony does not play. Instead of concluding, as Gay's Beggar had done, that 'the lower sort of people have their vices in a degree as well as the rich', Fielding suggests in *Jonathan Wild* that the lower sort of people, such as the Heartfrees, have virtues which too often pass unrecognized: the 'low' virtues of tenderness, honesty, and affection. The use of mock-heroic here is quite different from that in *Tom Thumb*;

[1] See W. R. Irwin, *The Making of Jonathan Wild* (New York, 1941).

like George Lillo (whose domestic tragedy *Fatal Curiosity*
Fielding had praised in 1736 for its sympathetic portrayal
of 'lower life'),[1] Fielding is in fact implicitly suggesting in
Jonathan Wild that it is perhaps time that literature began
to address itself towards certain areas of life which have
been traditionally considered beneath its dignity.

It is Fielding's cheerful trust in the basic worthiness of
low life which makes *Jonathan Wild* a very different work
from *The Beggar's Opera*. Like *The Modern Husband* (1732),
in which Fielding had pitted the low but honest Mr. Bella-
mant against the high but wicked Lord Richly, and like
Amelia, with its constant simple contrasts between love-
in-a-cottage and love-in-a-palace, *Jonathan Wild* is fundamentally a sentimental work. The direction of Fielding's
irony, unlike the direction of Gay's, is always comfortably
predictable. Fielding's use of the animal analogy, for
instance, is markedly different from Gay's: a good-natured
man is like a little fish in a pike-pond (II. i); 'What a wolf
is in a sheepfold, a GREAT MAN is in society' (IV. iii). There
is no possibility, as there was in *The Beggar's Opera*, that the
little fish might turn out to be predatory itself, or that the
sheep might unexpectedly bite the wolf; those who are
wicked are wicked and those who are not are not. For-
tunately there are plenty of those who are not. The famous
passage about 'employing hands' (I. xiv) flings its irony at
'conquerors', 'absolute princes', 'statesmen', and 'prigs',
but reassuringly suggests that 'the yeoman, the manu-
facturer, the merchant, and perhaps the gentleman' are all
usefully working on behalf of the national good. The two
lists are very reasonably drawn up; there is nothing here to
ruffle or disconcert, as there was in Swift's list of lawyer,
pickpocket, and colonel. And consequently as a work of
satire *Jonathan Wild* has no real cutting edge; it is in this

[1] See Fielding's prologue to *Fatal Curiosity*.

case the absence of 'total irony' which results in insipidity. Once again Fielding's irony and his optimism seem to stand curiously at odds with each other. On the one hand, Fielding implies, as he had done in *The Author's Farce* and in *Pasquin*, that public affairs in England are organized as blatantly as in a puppet-show, and that contemporary life is as absurd as a theatrical farce. On the other hand, *Jonathan Wild* does not end at all absurdly. 'Providence', acting in the best traditions of stage comedy, brings the Heartfrees through their many trials to a happy reunion, even finally restoring to Mrs. Heartfree her stolen jewels. Jonathan Wild meets with 'the proper catastrophe of a GREAT MAN' and 'with universal applause' swings out of the world. Virtue is rewarded and vice is punished, and affairs return once more to order.

To bring a play or a novel to a happy conclusion is normally to imply that you think that, given certain terms, life itself is likely to turn out happily. One obvious way of moderating such an implication is to be a bit perfunctory about one's ending, as Jonson, Wycherley, and Gay (as we have seen) each were at times, in their different ways. In *The Beggar's Opera*, for instance, Gay implies that the reprieve which comes to Macheath is a preposterous and improbable literary patch-up, the last sign of the farcical nature of the times. 'So, now the whole thing has a happy end!' exclaims Mrs. Peachum in Brecht's version of the play: 'How calm and peaceful would our life be always if a messenger came from the king whenever we wanted.' In *Jonathan Wild* Fielding also supplies a last-minute reprieve as a part of the final, happy movement of the story, but his emphasis is very different from Gay's. In *The Beggar's Opera* the reprieve arrives absurdly for the man who actually deserves (and wants) to hang; in *Jonathan Wild* it arrives very justly to release the innocent Heartfree. In *The Beggar's Opera* the reprieve arrives because of the Player's feeling

that the play should conform to an artificial convention of
the theatre; on the other hand, says Fielding disarmingly
to the reader of *Jonathan Wild*, '. . . lest our reprieve should
seem to resemble that in the *Beggar's Opera*, I shall endeavour
to show him that this incident, which is undoubtedly true,
is at least as natural as delightful; for we assure him we
would rather have suffered half mankind to be hanged than
have saved one contrary to the strictest rules of writing and
probability.' 'At least as natural as delightful': Fielding is
smiling, but more than half-believes it; in real life such happy
turns of fortune are not impossible. And he follows up the
proposition with a quick joke stolen from Molière: 'It
is better to die through following the rules,' declares the
doctor in *L'Amour Médecin*, 'than to recover through violat-
ing them.' Fielding repeats the joke in *Tom Jones* (XVII. i)
when he speculates about Tom's chances of escaping the
gallows: 'If he doth not, therefore, find some natural means
of fairly extricating himself from all his distresses, we will
do no violence to the truth and dignity of our history for
his sake; for we had rather relate that he was hanged at
Tyburn (which may very probably be the case) than forfeit
our integrity, or shock the faith of our reader.' The eventual
happy outcome of Tom's story is, once more, seen as both
providential and 'natural'—Tom is (to use Fielding's phrase)
fairly extricated from his misfortunes. The comic ending is
very stubborn in Fielding's work, and it is not surprising
that in two recent adaptations of *Tom Jones* for film and stage
the time-hallowed device of a last-minute reprieve (which
is not present in the novel) should have been used to resolve
the action. It may be noticed in passing that Defoe had
handled the final reprieve of Moll Flanders as she lay in Newgate with a comparable, if somewhat sterner, insistence on
the probability of such events occurring in real life. Many
people, says Moll, would like to hear that she had been

hanged: 'Such, however, will, I hope, allow me liberty to make my story complete. It would be a severe satire on such to say they do not relish the repentence as much as they do the crime; and they had rather the history were a complete tragedy, as it was very likely to have been.'[1] Life can and does turn out happily. Fielding, like Defoe, insists upon this in *Jonathan Wild* and in all his other novels, and it is this insistence which most obviously marks Fielding off from the older generation of satirists.

One further small point should be noticed in connection with the reprieve at the end of *Jonathan Wild*. Its arrival is 'natural' because (unknown to the reader) the thing has been engineered some time before by a sharp-witted and conscientious Justice of the Peace. The presence of this J.P.—he is called, simply, 'the good magistrate'—is of some importance to the ending of the story; Fielding keeps him on the scene for several more chapters, although he has nothing much to do except to listen sympathetically to Mrs. Heartfree's tale of her adventures. Yet his presence is a quiet reminder that corruption is not universal, that the laws of the land are basically benign and workable, and that through the offices of such men as this they can be made to prevail. Towards the end of her story, Mrs. Heartfree tells of an encounter she has had in Africa with another kind of magistrate, and goes on to describe in some detail how such men are regarded in that country: they are chosen for their superior bravery and wisdom; in office, their power is absolute, but they can be deposed and punished for the slightest deviation in the use of that power; they are deeply venerated, yet they are also regarded as the people's slaves, and must always be accessible to complainants. They also wear rings in their noses, and each evening are gently kicked, in private, by a kind of beadle, to school them in

---

[1] *Moll Flanders*, Everyman edition (London, 1930), p. 251.

humility. (This particular magistrate, like everyone else in the story, is also attracted by Mrs. Heartfree's virtue, and makes an unsuccessful cash offer for it.) The incident is odd, and at first sight quite gratuitous. One supposes that Fielding had *Gulliver's Travels* somewhere at the back of his mind as he wrote, but his emphasis is quite un-Swiftian: this glimpse into the manners and laws of another country is not intended to arouse in us any real doubts about the way things work in England, or to diminish our admiration of the good magistrate who has come to Heartfree's rescue. It serves rather to remind us of the importance of judges in general; of the fact that, while they are men like everyone else, they also earn the dignity in which they are conventionally held, for the law is our only final safeguard against the kind of criminality and deviousness which has been the central subject of the book. With the introduction of the good magistrate at the end of *Jonathan Wild*, and this subtle endorsement of his importance, Fielding is at a delicate point of transition, bringing his story back into the world of law and order. This point of transition is similar to that in the final act of *Rape Upon Rape* (1730), where Fielding introduces Justice Worthy to untangle the play's confusions and, by his very presence, to reassure us that not all magistrates are like the unspeakable Mr. Squeezum. And behind Justice Worthy lies a long line of good magistrates who traditionally appear, like Jonson's Justice Clement, at the end of a comedy to resolve the confusions of the previous acts, to adjudicate over rival claims, to bring the world gently back the right way up. Fielding is particularly concerned with this concluding movement of comedy, both in his plays and in his novels, being careful to lead us back from a world of Saturnalian confusions to a world of law and order; and it is for this reason that his inversions of high and low in *Jonathan Wild* carry quite different implications from Gay's superficially similar inversions in *The Beggar's Opera*, and that we may describe him as being, in a technical sense, a more purely comic artist than Gay.

The crucial problem in Fielding's work becomes that of relating the egalitarian world of comedy with the hierarchical world of actual life. In his Preface to *Joseph Andrews* Fielding makes it clear that he regards his old methods of burlesque—'appropriating the manners of the highest to the lowest, or *è converso*'—as finally irresponsible: for 'we should ever confine ourselves strictly to Nature'. Fielding's new species of writing is to be modelled not on burlesque but (amongst other things) upon the traditions of 'the comic' —and Fielding goes on to pay tribute to Ben Jonson's unrivalled success in this mode. In *Joseph Andrews* and *Tom Jones* the high and the low are still brought into comparison with each other, but in an altogether gentler and more tolerant way. It is necessary for a writer, Fielding argues in *Tom Jones* (ix. i) to know all walks of life, to see it steadily and see it whole:

> Now this conversation in our historian must be universal, that is, with all ranks and degrees of men; for the knowledge of what is called high life will not instruct him in low; nor, *è converso*, will his being acquainted with the inferior part of mankind teach him the manners of the superior. And though it may be thought that the knowledge of either may sufficiently enable him to describe at least that in which he hath been conversant, yet he will even here fall greatly short of perfection; for the follies of either rank do in reality illustrate each other.

'The follies of either rank do in reality illustrate each other': it is for this reason that Fielding objects in *Tom Jones* (v. i) that the 'modern judges of our theatres' have rejected what is known as the 'low' in comedy—'by which they have happily succeeded in banishing all humour from the stage, and have made the theatre as dull as a drawing-room!'

Dr. Johnson complained that *Tom Jones* was 'of very low life', and Richardson that Tom was 'the lowest of all fellows',[1] yet Fielding's real concern was to draw together both low and high in gentle ironical comparison. The apparent egalitarianism of his comedy is not so much satirical as Christian, and Fielding follows, like Parson Adams, the example 'of him who made no distinction, unless, peradventure, by preferring the poor to the rich' (*Joseph Andrews*, III. ii). Dr. Harrison in *Amelia* criticizes 'the custom of the world; which instead of being formed on the precepts of our religion to consider each other as brethren, teaches us to regard those who are a degree below us, either in rank or fortune, as a species of being of an inferior order in creation' (IX. v). Fielding's mature comedy, I have suggested in the first chapter, is often the comedy of unexpected brotherhood, in which quite dissimilar people suddenly and surprisingly find themselves related. Parson Adams calls Parson Trulliber his 'brother' and sets off a train of misunderstandings (II. xiv); and *Joseph Andrews* ends, as does *Tom Jones*, with a stress upon a new and more literal kind of brotherhood: Squire Booby explains to Lady Booby that his marriage to Pamela has affected the way in which Joseph, too, must be regarded: 'It is true her brother hath been your servant, but he is now become my brother; and I have one happiness, that neither his character, his behaviour or appearance, give me any reason of being ashamed of calling him so' (IV. v).

Fielding's levelling of high and low may often suggest that the terms are traditionally misapplied—'High people signify no other than people of fashion', he writes in *Joseph Andrews* (II. xiii), 'and low people those of no fashion'—

---

[1] *Boswell's Life of Johnson*, ed. Hill/Powell, ii. 174; *Selected Letters of Samuel Richardson*, ed. John Carroll (Oxford, 1964), p. 127 (letter to Astraea and Minerva Hill, 4 August 1749).

but not that such distinctions are fundamentally unnecessary. His comedy rests upon a double standard, that class distinctions are, and are not, important. It is the double standard of Parson Adams, who at the end of *Joseph Andrews* (IV. xvi) rebukes Mr. Booby and Pamela for laughing in church, and 'would have done no less to the highest prince on earth: for tho' he paid all submission and deference to his superiors in other matters, where the least spice of religion intervened, he immediately lost all respect of persons'. Despite the fact that Booby is rebuked by Adams, it is remarkable with what care Fielding also rehabilitates him in this ultimate section of the novel, establishing him as a kindly and benevolent landed gentleman, whose hospitality and wealth ease the story towards its thoroughly happy conclusion; if he is a booby he is also a squire. Fielding is bringing us back from the world in which each man is as good as his brother to a world in which the role and function of the landed gentry may be tactfully endorsed. A less smooth transition occurs at the end of *Tom Jones* at a moment whose complexity has been admirably discussed by Empson:[1] that at which Tom is rebuked by Allworthy for wanting to forgive Black George for having stolen his banknote. It is almost (Empson suggests) as if Fielding implies that the Sermon on the Mount, if observed punctiliously, would result in social anarchy, as if Fielding the magistrate had momentarily triumphed over Fielding the Christian; social order seems to be of greater importance than perfect forgiveness. The moment is curious, certainly, and it is also of some wider interest; by his explicitness at this point, Fielding highlights an element which is often present at the end of comedy, though usually more tactfully concealed. ('Think not on him till tomorrow', says Benedick, learning at the end of *Much Ado* of the

[1] William Empson, '*Tom Jones*', *The Kenyon Review*, xx (1958), pp. 217–49.

capture of Don John: 'I'll devise thee brave punishments for him.') We are used to the notion that comedy ends in lovers' meetings, with promises of marriage and the arrival of unexpected fortunes, with general reconciliations and forgivenesses, with dances, feasting, and widely-bestowed goodwill. Fielding's work, as we have seen, characteristically moves to a conclusion of this kind, a conclusion which is normally devoid of major irony or pessimism or sense of imminent doom. Yet as we have also seen, the generally happy ending of comedy may also at times barely manage to conceal another harsher feeling, of returning sobriety and returning awareness of the demands of law and order, of the fact that the levelling and revelling must soon come to a stop, that the world must move once more the right way up. In Fielding's work the 'sense of an ending' is often of this kind: though events move magically towards their resolution, the hard paradoxes remain; benevolence is good, but so is prudence; mercy is good, but so is judgement; all men are flesh and blood, all men are brothers, but some must rule over others. Two incompatible worlds continue to exert their sharply different attractions for us right to the end.

INDEX

PRINTED IN GREAT BRITAIN
AT THE UNIVERSITY PRESS, OXFORD
BY VIVIAN RIDLER
PRINTER TO THE UNIVERSITY